ANYWHERE BUT HERE

How Our **Left Hemisphere** *Distracts Our Awareness from Our* **True Self**

A Personal View by
MARK PIFER

Text copyright © 2012 Mark Pifer
All Rights Reserved

ISBN: 1-4783-3668-4
ISBN-13: 9781478336686

ANYWHERE BUT HERE

How Our **Left Hemisphere** *Distracts Our Awareness from Our* **True Self**

A Personal View by
MARK PIFER

*Dedicated to: Richard,
for all your years of patience
and your unfailing faith in me.*

*I don't know how I came to deserve your guidance.
I am so blessed to have met you.*

*There is no book or peace
without your patient and gentle teaching
over these many years.*

*I am now and will forever remain,
your grateful student.*

Contents

Intro 1
   Why I Wrote This Book 3
   On Human Perception and Liberation 5
   A Caution to Zealots 7
   The Short Version 9
This Didn't Come From Out Of Nowhere 11
A Part of the Whole 17
   A Quivering Feeling 19
   Karma (Conditioned Reality) 21
   The Need to Be Seen 22
How We Got Here 23
The Frontal Lobe 29
Two Hemispheres of our Brain 33
   The Two Sages 35
   Why We Need Two Perceptions 40
How Our Hemispheres Perceive 43
The Left Hemisphere 47
Evaluation Functions 51
   Problem Solving, The Barrier Between You and Peace ... 54
Symbolic Language 59
   Let Go of Pointers 63
Time Sense 65
The Ego 69
The Story Teller 75
   The Tale of the Bad Posture 77
Beliefs & Certainty 83
   Why We Need Two Hemispheres and Certainty 88

    Anticipation and Reward 90
    Even Christ Had To Let Go Of Beliefs 92
Roles 93
The Limbic System 97
Limbic Conditioning (a.k.a. Pain Body) 101
The Right Hemisphere 105
A Non Judgmental Viewing Space (Accepting What Is).................... 109
The Present Moment..113
A Sense of Belonging 117
    The Bubble's Journey..119
Joy and Wonder.. 123
    Left Prefrontal Cortex...127
Fearlessness and Adventuresome Spirit 129
Non Clinging Sense of Love... 133
    Simple Reflection.. 135
Intuitive Sense of "Knowing" 137
Common Left Hemisphere Strategies to Maintain Conditioning 143
    What Does The Ego Want? 145
    Anywhere But Here 145
    "Yeah, yeah, I've already heard this before…" 148
    What's the Point? 148
    Fighting the Fire While Feeding the Flame 149
    Seeking Salvation in Time 150
    But, it's true… 151
    Specialness 152
    Warping "Accept What Is" 154
    Chasing Past Spiritual Experiences.. 154
    The "Ah-ha" Trap 155
    Conceptualizing A Spiritual Method 156
    Chasing External Sources...157
    Grim Seriousness and Negative Evaluations 158
    The Loudest Voice 159

A Special Trap For Spiritual (especially Adviata - or "Non Dualism") Students 161
The Loud Drunk 163
How to De-Stimulate Limbic Conditioning (and Pain Body Strategies) 165
90 Seconds To Peace 168
On hallucinogens and the Pineal Gland 168
How to Stimulate Right Hemisphere Functions 171
How To Enter the Right Hemisphere...............................173
The Method 175
Through The Senses...175
4 Basic Meditation Techniques 176
The Process 179
Blood Flow 181
The Wave and the Ocean Metaphor Unveiled.............. 182
Forgive, Accept, Release, Relax... 185
Counter "Intuitive" 188
Forgive...191
Accept... 195
Release 199
Relax 203
Deconditioning Takes Time, and it can only happen in the Now 207
The Journey 209
Unraveling a conditioned behavior................................. 209
Enlightened Relationships..213
Difficult and Deeply Unconscious People 215
What No One Tells You 216
No, with love 216
Be The Change...217
Some Essays 219
The Present Is Freedom...221
How to Ride the Now..221
The Left Hemisphere Tool in This Search 223

10 Enlightenment Commandments 224
The Most Common "Sins" of Religious Practitioners 232
Satsangs (Q&A With Viewers) 237
   Female (Age 21) 239
   Male (Age 23) 289
   Male (Age 17) 311
   Singular Questions 322
Disclaimer 335

Intro

*"I appeal to you with my folded hands,
don't get into this spirituality.
Whatever knowledge and concepts you are having,
only that final spark is to be applied.
You have everything, the raw material is already with you,
the symbol of birth and death is already removed.
The factual state of affairs is open, very clear,
but nobody wants to look at it."*

- Nisargadatta Maharaj

Why I Wrote This Book

I sat in my bed at night with one small thought, in the form of a prayer. Prayers were new to me being an atheist for most of my adult life, but I felt few options. I begged. I pleaded. I cried and wept the most simple and direct prayer I could think of:

"Please God, let me die in my sleep tonight..."

Dreams were torture and waking was worse. There was no escape from the misery and the deep feelings of loss and disgust with life.

My family members and friends either avoided me completely or stammered and searched for helpful phrases to try in vain to "lift my spirits." I could hear the fear in their voices. A few close family members made it simple:

"If you kill yourself, you will hurt me deeply..."

Hence the prayer.

"Please God, let me die in my sleep tonight..."

That way, we're all happy. I end the misery and they can't say that I did it to myself to hurt them. It's a win/win scenario. My father even hinted at having my freedom taken from me by institutionalizing me. The threat of adding even more horror and pain to my horrible situation was not an incentive to stick around awhile and figure it out. That threat made the feeling MUCH more imminent and necessary, kill myself BEFORE the men in white coats showed up and my life fell into a hell that I can't even begin to imagine where I'm kept alive so that my family didn't feel guilty about doing "nothing" and my misery was even more intensified by confinement. So I prayed:

"Please God, let me die in my sleep tonight..."

When I could no longer stand it I wrote a letter to my friends and family saying "Goodbye, I love you" in an attempt to get them to understand why they needed to let me go. I had been the student of a spiritual teacher for many years and my understanding of the material was quite profound, though completely intellectual. The end result of my conceptual understanding of the nature of reality was a nihilistic deadness that made every aspect of living feel numb, boring, and meaningless. I included my spiritual teacher in the list of recipients of my "goodbye e-mail" and his response when I called him the next day was quite shocking. The moment he heard my voice he said:

"I'm sure the letter you sent to your family and friends was quite disturbing to them. I on the other hand am excited at the prospect that you've finally had enough suffering and are ready to do the work..."

And I was struck dumb. You see it had simply never occurred to me, even though he repeatedly urged me otherwise, that I had never actually applied what I had learned in the texts. I had spent years gathering information into my brain as if the act alone would transfer the wisdom to my life through some sort of intellectual osmosis and never, even once, questioned whether the purely intellectual process was actually bringing peace and grace into my life. And so, with nothing to lose, I agreed, finally, to do the work and the book you are reading is the result of a merging of more study and finally, yes, finally the implementation of practice of what I've learned in my daily life. You see, other than my own naturally intellectual tendencies, what allowed me to "keep it intellectual" was the fact that all the language of the time was metaphorical and poetic. There was nothing specific for my mind to grasp onto as a process. Simultaneously, however, there were HUNDREDS of Gurus and Teachers who claimed they had the answers and methods personally. And, while my spiritual teacher was clearly a peaceful and very insightful fellow, I would allow myself to "critique" him with absurdly impossible standards held against his very human existence and allow myself, from those criticisms, to "let myself off the hook" and not "do the work" he had insisted I do for many years. In short, I allowed my mind to lure me, time and time again, away from doing work that it feared would cause its demise. I had certainly read time and time again about how "the mind" was the "problem" and needed to be transcended, etc., etc., but, what the hell was "the mind" anyway!?

At that time my teacher added to the list of material the works of Eckhart Tolle and I then found Dr. Jill Bolte Taylor's book "My Stroke Of Insight" and the addition of those two influences to my already well informed data pool launched my understanding into a whole new level.

Then, most importantly, I began my practice. The most simple and direct practice. And now, each day, I live in a state of peace. Now, when disrupted by thoughts and old conditioned patterns of behavior, I let go of them easily and come back to my peace at a moment's notice no matter what is happening in my life. In short, I no longer need external sources for my contentment or joy. I strongly recommend that you join me where everyone can go, to your birthright as human beings, to the peace and serenity that is your true nature.
Namaste

On Human Perception and Liberation

Every perception that we experience as a human being is filtered through the functions of our brains. When we perceive the universe, many different "possible" views are available depending on what brain functions are dominating the perception process at that moment. For instance, if our Amygdala fires, (part of the Limbic System of our brains) it narrows future responses because the function of the Amygdala is to assess incoming stimuli as "potentially dangerous" and then assign a fear(flight) or rage(fight) response to it. By doing so, it precludes many other brain functions from "having a go" at perceiving the experience. It, in a sense, hijacks the experience, and forces it down certain channels and away from others. And, it gets first crack at incoming stimuli, so you can see how important this particular brain function is in terms of how we perceive our experiences of the world. And this is just ONE brain function out of many that "compete" for your worldview, or more accurately, compete for how your brain is going to interpret incoming stimuli. We strengthen our brain functions through where we place our awareness (or where we "focus our attention" - the ability for the brain to re-wire to the demands of new environments, behaviors, etc. is called "neuroplasticity") and that tells the brain what sections to send the oxygen rich blood and "feed." And all sections of your brain want only one thing when they get fed, and that's MORE. The brain is a very competitive place, and the object of the competition is oxygen rich blood. The portions of your brain that get fed get stronger, larger, and the Neural Net grows and intertwines into other sections of the brain and begins to "color" your world view. And, again, the way in which we direct the blood flow is through where we place our awareness, coming to know the power of your own awareness is the key to all spiritual growth. If we focus our awareness in the past and future, stories, or evaluations we will feed the "adversarially separate" Left Hemisphere of our brains. If we give anger and fear a lot of attention we will feed the Amygdala (part of the Limbic System or "pain body") and we will suffer under the darkness it brings. If we focus on the present moment, the feelings of our inner body, or the input through our senses we feed the peaceful Right Hemisphere and gain all the benefits that come with it. In the end it's all up to us.

The dilemma is, that we are born with these brains, but there is no "owner's manual" to consult. After a time, we just assume that "how we perceive the world" is just "who we are" and there is no way to change this process. And there is nothing farther from the truth than this misconception. And many thousands of years ago, many wizened sages noticed this truth themselves and transformed (liberated) their lives from the confinements of their conditioned responses to incoming stimuli. And that is what this book is about. It's a look at how we can "liberate" ourselves from the conditioning that was handed to us, without our consent, by our DNA, childhoods, and environments. And how we can, through better knowledge about "how this stuff works" liberate ourselves from our previous conditioning and enjoy the peace and bliss that is our birthright. As we Abide in our True Selves in a state of

Nirvana:Nir·va·na/nərˈvänə/noun

1. A transcendent state in which there is neither suffering, desire, nor sense of self, and the subject is released from the effects of...

Another term that is often used in spiritual communities is the term "enlightenment." There are many existing definitions, some speak of it as a state that one achieves after many years of "spiritual work" others

speak of it in their own terms. When I speak of the term I me
follows:

En·light·en·ment/en'lītnmənt/noun

1. The "lightening" (reduction) of our conceptual overlay of reality as it is.

This book is not going to be an all encompassing look at brain functions, the material of this book is tailored specifically to the purpose of Liberation. I hope it serves you, and through it you can come to a point where the nagging and painful sense that this moment in your life is "not enough" or "needs more" or "should be otherwise" is quieted and you are able to abide in your Self, right here, right now, which is where you always already are.

A Caution to Zealots

Zeal·ot /'zelət/

Noun: 1. A person who is fanatical and uncompromising in pursuit of their religious, political, or other ideals.

This book MIGHT be frustrating to the spiritual or scientific zealot.

The Scientific Zealot might be "put off" by the practical nature of this book or by the frequent usage of "poetic language" or "metaphors" about a subject normally the sole domain of science. The Scientific Zealot might be unsatisfied by the many conclusions drawn as practical pointers without extensive experimental testing, and also by the lack of a three letter acronym at the end of the author's name. And because it's a predominantly spiritual subject matter, they might take offense to academic subject matter being applied to "hocus pocus" or "mumbo-jumbo" practices. And, to those who feel they have been fighting a worldview dominated by religious radicalism, they might fear a "slipping back" to a time when people like Galileo could be imprisoned for daring to go against the uncompromising theocracy that dominated times past. In short, there might be fear of losing society's perception of science as the "modern authority" of all things known and to be known and a blending of scientific and spiritual material might be viewed as a threat to that perception.

The Spiritual Zealot might be "put off" by the inclusion of science in what was once a completely spiritual domain (liberation practices.) They might find the inclusion of neuroscientific material to be an inference that there are no "mystical" or "otherworldly" explanations to the practice of liberation from one's ego (that it's "all in the brain..." etc.)   They might feel that introducing science into the realm of the metaphysical will somehow be a threat to their previous monopoly on the religious practice of "liberation from one's ego." If they make their living as a "spiritual guide/teacher" they might view an inclusion of science as a threat to their pocket books. They might see scientific explanations for their teachings and practices as a reduction of the subject matter to the base or material world and find such limitations to be a threat to supernatural authority figure(s) who usually grant "spiritual powers" to a chosen few...

But for the rest of us, who live in the modern world and inherently see flaws in a dogmatic approach to clinging to one OR the other "worldview" the merging of scientific and spiritual subjects might be a portal through which they can finally embrace material that for many years had sounded either "too dry and analytical" or "too fluffy and fantastical" and maybe, just maybe, find that a blend of the two approaches was similar to Goldilocks' "just right" for a pathway to liberation from the suffering (or what the Buddha called "dukkha") that often comes from the manner in which our brains tend to interpret stimuli and project painful and limiting conclusions based on repetitive previous evaluations onto the perception of the world at large.

It is my sincere hope that this book speaks to you and in some way offers even the slightest relief from what can begin as a wonderful tool but in most cases turn into a cage of suffering that we hold between our ears and offers you some insight into how you can tune into your more peaceful wiring, and bring that peace and joy into your life and the lives of those around you and the world at large.

The Short Version

Here is the whole book, in fact here is all of spirituality in a nutshell. You need no more than this:

There is no past or future. They are products of your mind and can only be experienced as thoughts in the present moment. YOU cannot exist outside of this present moment. Therefore you ARE what happens to you in this present moment. Enlightenment, Liberation, Nirvana, the Atman, Christ or Buddha Nature, is the merging of your awareness with who you ARE. Therefore when you merge your awareness with what you ARE now, you are liberated.

Standing in the way of this is years of conditioning that compel you to look:

Anywhere But Here

Once you see that YOU are always HERE, you can then see clearly that that conditioning is not YOU. Once you see that, you can begin, through simply watching it but not engaging in it, to re-wire your brain to BE HERE NOW. And there are many fine ways of accessing that wiring, which is housed in the Right Hemisphere of your brain. In time you will no longer run the old conditioned wiring and you will Abide in the Self, which is always here. And in that space, that is always YOU, there is a great peace and bliss.

That's it, now please go and do likewise.

Namaste.

OR, if you find that you need more convincing, read the rest of this book (and/or many other books), until you have the courage to be who you are.

This Didn't Come From Out Of Nowhere

*"But I'll tell you what hermits realize.
If you go off into a far, far forest and get very quiet,
you'll come to understand that you're
connected with everything."*

- Alan Watts

In almost all of the major religions there is a person who came to some amazing realizations about their place in the universe. It usually followed some time alone in deep introspection and resulted in a message that they wanted to share with the world. And it is highly improbable to believe that all of the beautiful sentiments found in the many religious/spiritual texts came from knowingly disingenuous sources. Clearly those who were writing about the mystical/spiritual experiences that they felt firsthand and through which insights like *"Do unto others as you would have done to yourself"* came from experienced SOMETHING. Thousands of years worth of material has been written by many sources, many voices, and they have all been very similar: from Christianity's *"Love thy neighbor as thyself"* to Buddhism's *"One who, while himself seeking happiness, oppresses with violence other beings who also desire happiness, will not attain happiness hereafter"* or Hinduism's *"One should never do that to another which one regards as injurious to one's own self. This, in brief, is the rule of dharma. Other behavior is due to selfish desires"* we hear echoes of the same messages, messages of a feeling of unity with others, with the world, and the universe at large. For those many thousands of years the people who were the sources of these words had only the use of poetic metaphorical language to discuss their shifts of perception, that is, until the direct experience of Dr. Jill Bolte Taylor who, through her "Stroke of Insight" came to know that all humans possess these perceptions and they can access them through a hemispherical perception shift, i.e. a shift from primary Left Hemispherical Perception to Primary Right Hemispherical Perception. Dr. Taylor's experience through the Right Hemisphere echoes those many voices of the past that urged us to find a way to let go of the feeling of being separate isolated "selves" in a sea of potential competitors who are "out to take what is ours" to Dr. Taylor's description of:

> ***"A world filled with beautiful peaceful compassionate loving people who knew that they could come to this space at any time and that they could purposely choose to step to the right of their Left Hemispheres and find this peace..."***

And, while the competitive worldview has been useful in an evolutionary sense for many millions of years, it's time that it's put to rest and a new worldview take its place. This view is echoed in the words of Dr. Stephen Hawking who when he cautioned:

> *"...our genetic code still carries selfish and aggressive instincts that were a survival advantage in the past..."*

was making a plea that we as a species find a way to work toward a solution to this evolutionarily induced epidemic or in the words of Eckhart Tolle:

> *"Another hundred years of the old egoic (Left Hemispheric) consciousness that has created the history of the 20th century which is mad, the planet will not be able to survive another 100 years of that madness."*

The knowledge alone is not enough, for it's not enough to know this intellectually, this is a philosophy that has to be lived and practiced. The Left Hemisphere (or The "Ego" in Spiritual terms) is not going to give up control without a fight.

So, my highest priority here is to highlight the functioning of this wonderful navigational tool we've inherited through birth called the human brain. It doesn't come with an instruction manual and has, built into it, some perceptions that were very necessary in our evolutionary development when we were fighting other species for "domination" of this wonderful ball of rock and water we were born onto. Separation, aggression, anger, fear, intellectual manipulation of natural environments, these all were very important to the propagation of the species, and the development of our language centers, frontal lobes, and left hemispherical functions were primary in that competitive need. However, now that we've reached the 7,000,000,000 population mark, that competitive need has clearly passed and it's past time to switch our world views to a more peaceful, loving, and unified approach. And while there are many cultural examples of peaceful, loving, and natural worldviews that existed and thrived (many Native American Tribes come to mind as well as the Bushman of the Kalahari Desert to name a few...) we seem, through natural selection (as well as dominant aggressive cultures taking over control of the planet) to have "naturally selected" ourselves away from the unified approach and now are leaning FAR too heavily on outdated aggressive wiring that is going to continue to cause pain and suffering on this planet until we find methods of regaining access to our more peaceful brain circuitry. So I'm here to share with the world what I have learned from my personal practice and study that might prove useful as information about the reader's own internal wiring so they can operate the "vehicles" they've inherited better, better not just for themselves, but for the planet and the species at large. I won't tell you that in the future I will agree with every word in this book, but it's the best I have to offer to date. And I can vouch from my personal experience that the study and more importantly practice of this material has had a profoundly peaceful and blissful effect on my daily life and that of those around me. In short, it's a combination of what I learned from the study of spiritual texts and my understanding of the science of the present. It's a twofold approach to the problem of the egoic (Left Hemispherical) worldview and the pain and suffering it causes both ourselves and others on a daily basis. It's time for us to ease that pain, and finally rid ourselves from the painful misconceptions and delusions that come from seeing everyone and everything around us as potential enemies and competitors. And to quote Bodhidharma a 6th century Zen Master:

*"**Not creating** delusions **is enlightenment**..."*

A Part of the Whole

*"I am made from the dust of the stars
and the oceans flow in my veins . . ."*

- Neil Peart

We are all made from the same energy that exploded from the Big Bang and made its way to the present moment to form our bodies. Every last bit of what we perceive to be us was once crafted in the heart of a star and released into the universe after its demise in a large explosion sending its dust travelling through space to join with other stardust and create wonderful and fascinating objects. I'd like to share a piece I wrote about this in a more "spiritual" metaphorical style of writing:

A Quivering Feeling

From the pit of my stomach comes a quivering feeling. The entire universe, every bit of energy within it is composed of the same source material: string theory, animating energy, cosmic consciousness, or even God. There is only this present moment and when we notice it it's like stepping out of the theater and having "real" sensations for the first time after being immersed in the fantasy of the dark movie theater and the images that felt so real on the screen that when the hero was in danger we felt it; in the middle of our stomachs, a quivering feeling. If everything is God, then so is the quivering feeling and the perception of it and the idea that the two are separate, and so am I, we are all God. And if that is so, then there is certainly nothing to fear. Why should one fear oneself? The fear, which is also God, is generated when one clings to this form, this body, this perceived life. When we decide to place value on this body we have decided to place value on one small amount of energy in the vast ocean of the universe. This is a losing proposition and the deck is highly stacked against the view. The universe will out. Your perceived body is a part of that universe and as a member of Everything - of God - it is safe and loved and a part of a grand whole. When you covet it and like a child and scream "mine" you create an artificial value on it that the universe doesn't share. And yet, the artificial value is ALSO God. God deciding to create bias for one form and play a game with itself. The game is identifying with that one small bit of energy in the vast ocean. Watching the movie in one's head of one wave heading toward the shore to crash and disperse, and being highly conscious of its doom. Of course, once it crashes onto the shore, it merely dissipates and falls back into the ocean whence it came, really where it never left, but while its headed to the shore the intense drama one feels and the quivering feeling in one's stomach are all exciting and entertaining. The ocean as a whole is just too vast, too deep, too beyond simple brain function to fathom clearly and therefore to a brain, useless. But the wave! The wave is easy to understand. We can watch as it's born off the shore and as it builds to its peak, and as it does it gives the outward impression that it might never stop building! And then it begins to break, and it's the first implication that its existence is finite. Its form is an illusion. Even with this understanding we cling to the form of the wave and ignore the calm depths beneath it. But what an entertaining game! God entertaining God by forgetting that the entire ocean is God! God can enjoy the quivering sensation in the stomach, because the narrowness of that perception creates a sensation that God would not have as the entire ocean. The entire ocean KNOWS that the wave is safe and simply a part of itself, with nowhere to go that will ultimately return to the whole body once it crashes to the shore. But narrowing one's focus to the wave, ah, what a game! What a way to pass the time as the endless silence of the ocean. Watching the wave like someone in a movie theater, aware that it's just an illusion but getting caught up in the moment to pass the time and lose oneself in the artificial drama. Ego identity is entertainment. Purposeful ignorance for an omniscient being who IS everything including the sensation of ignorance. God entertaining God. Creating puppets and hiding the strings from perception and then watching the show. Like a child playing with dolls. Making all the voices, creating drama for the dolls to act out, acting as if the dolls were individuals with egos and feelings when in fact there is only one source for all the sensations; the puppeteer. God entertaining God. God drives down the road and God, in the car behind God, pressures it to drive faster. Pushes the car dangerously close to the back of the other car, and God in the pressured car feels the pressure and gets angry at the callous and thoughtless God in the car behind. The plot of the movie thickens. Anger rises. Egos clash. The puppets fight and clash and create entertaining drama. And without the narrowed egoic perception, God could not experience it all "first hand" because the puppet show looks very different from above or behind where the puppeteer and the strings exist. The perception MUST artificially narrow to the small hole in the front of the box that obscures the puppeteer for the show to be effective. God has to identify through egoic consciousness with one small mind to be able to enjoy the show called human drama. Otherwise, strings showing, puppeteer's lips moving, the illusion is shattered. We are God's movie stars. Entertainment for infinity. And as such we are quite special.

Karma (Conditioned Reality)

There is nothing in this universe that isn't linked to the whole and therefore there are no individual parts that exist independently. Every bit of motion in this universe ripples out and touches the rest of the universe. It can be said that we, as part of the whole, are merely being rocked by the ripples of events that came before us. And then on top of those ripples we add our own and the new karma moves out away from us to other destinations. Of course, one of those destinations must, because we are a part of the whole, be that the ripple's effect, now gathering more power through the influence of other ripples, returns to us with greater effect, and on and on we go. The ripples turn into waves, the waves turn into larger waves, until the tsunami wreaks its devastation...

If you wanted to see this effect manifested you could stand in a kiddy pool and start to make waves, as you splash about it won't take long for the waves to build upon one another and soon the kiddy pool will be unable to contain the entire process and water will splash everywhere.

So, what does this mean? How do we get out of this process? Well, to use the kiddy pool analogy, it's pretty simple, you step out of the kiddy pool. You find a way to let go of that which is creating the ripples. And the ripples, in time, calm, and become a clear and peaceful surface.

That's what we're going to discuss here, how we can step out of the pool, and let the ripples die down and become the peace that is always under the surface of the waves.

The Need to Be Seen

It is an innately human desire to want to be seen, moreover to be seen exactly as we are. More strongly, to be loved exactly as we are. Seeing something as it is and accepting it with our whole heart IS love. This drive is universal. We all come from the same energy that sprang from the big bang, and it all holds with it the same drive. To be seen, to be seen as it is. To be loved, to be loved as it is. This is why the whole point of this existence is to finally see the universe as it is. We're here to "wake up" it has been stated many times, what we're waking to is simply what is. To finally see the universe as it is and love it with our whole heart. That is the purpose of human consciousness, and the driving force of our existence.

How We Got Here

"Few people are capable of expressing with equanimity opinions which differ from the prejudices of their social environment. Most people are even incapable of forming such opinions."

- Albert Einstein

The human brain is our evolutionary strength. Its ability to morph its perceptions to the needs of the environment in which it was born is astoundingly powerful. When we are born our brains are very much like "blank slates" (there are genetic predispositions, but if they are never triggered by external stimuli, it will be the same as if they don't exist...) waiting for us to map them through the process of where we focus our attention, or in spiritual terms, where we place our awareness.

It took millions of years to create the human brain and each step was built upon a previously existing system and so our brains are built from a lower, very primal brain (often nicknamed the "reptilian brain") that filters incoming stimuli and attaches a "feeling" before passing it along to the upper (often nicknamed the "monkey brain") regions for "reasonable or cognitive thought." And because of this process, to quote Dr. Taylor:

"Although many of us may think of ourselves as thinking creatures that feel, biologically we are feeling creatures that think..."

So, each sensation that passes through our brain has both sensory data and a "feeling" attached to that data supplied to us from our Limbic System (or Reptilian Brain) which forms very early in our lives (as newborns) and wires at that time due to sensory stimuli and then does not mature (or change) as the brain ages, and so each "feeling" that it generates (and what kinds it tends to generate) is not much different at the age of fifty as it was at the age of two or twenty years old.

The two cerebral hemispheres of our brain also develop at different rates, with the Left Hemisphere developing first (hence establishing its dominance) in early childhood (ages 2 to 6), and the Right Hemisphere developing more fully in middle childhood (ages 7 to 11). The necessity of the Left Hemisphere developing first is due to the fact that our Language Centers are located within it and our need to learn speech is very important to how our brains are mapped as our development progresses.

This entire process is formed through where we, through environmental stimuli, focus our attention due to the tasks associated with the environmental needs. The cells of our brains, through repeated stimulation, in time no longer need external stimuli to activate, and will continue to function even when no external sources are present (like a heightened sense of smell for a farmer to "know" when his crops are ripe, or heightened sense of vision for hunters to track and spot prey, etc.) In short, these systems have been placed on "high priority" or "conditioned" and now run on their own. These high priority or conditioned systems are maintained when no external stimuli is present through the playing out of scenarios either past or fantasy based future visions through our Frontal Lobe brain functions. The Frontal Lobe is what allows us to recall memories in our heads of past experiences and is also where we watch "mental movies" or visions to stimulate high priority systems and keep them sharp and ready to fire when "needed." And the human brain holds no distinctions or predilections as to environments, it doesn't categorize our beginning environments as "good" or "bad" to the human brain the environment it was born into simply is, and that which it has never been exposed to, to it, simply doesn't exist. In short, the brain begins with no judgments, it merely accepts the environment it was born into and does the "best it can" with what it was given. And for modern man, that environment is very artificial and "crafted" and holds many unnatural necessities of behavior for the safety and well being of those who live within it. A special skill set is needed to survive in it and so parents are forced to teach modern children to have many, upon reflection, strange survival mechanisms that would to a naturally born person seem bizarre and even insane. That is why there are so many quotes from Native People over the years discussing the fact that the Western Man is "never satisfied" or "ever anxious" or "never still." We've brought ourselves to a place where stillness and peace no longer play a large role in our lives, and we are paying the price for this in terms of our stress, anxiety, and just plain suffering.

And so, from this we can see that a child's view is formed by their childhood environments and their attention, awareness, is drawn to behaviors that garnish their parent's (and other social stimuli's) approval and due to the fact that many of these behaviors are no longer (due to the necessities of survival in the "modern world") natural impulses the child quickly finds that they must "perform" (generate behavior that is not a natural response) to please the parent (or social authority.) This is the beginning of the formation of a "conceptual self" or "ego." Sadly, in time, even when we no longer need to interact with the environments that demanded the conceptually created self we forget that this conceptual self was just a tool for surviving our childhoods. We grow so used to it we see it as "ourselves" because we've worn the mask so long that we have completely forgotten our "true face" underneath it. It is that dynamic that ultimately leads to ego (Left Hemisphere – false self) addiction. Of course, if you don't need to please anyone to be fed any longer, you can let this go...

The Frontal Lobe

*"Don't take anything personally.
Nothing others do is because of you.
What others say and do is a projection
of their own reality, their own dream.
When you are immune to the opinions and actions of others,
you won't be the victim of needless suffering."*

- Miguel Ruiz

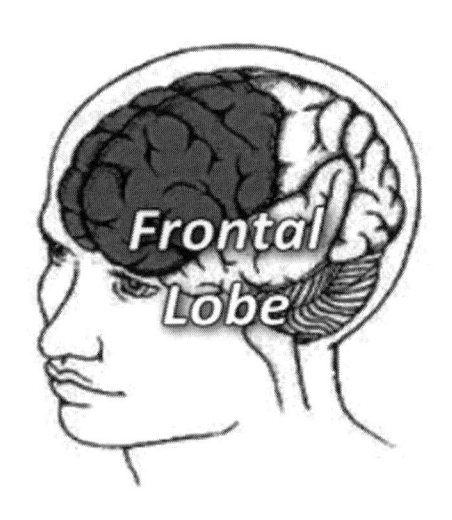

The development of the Frontal Lobe of our brains was a major change in our evolutionary structure and one of the last of all brain functions to come to full power (completing its maturation at about the age of 20.) The Frontal Lobe is primarily responsible for the monitoring of mental states and acts like a "control center" by rerouting our behavior toward more "civil" or "tempered" responses. And in fact much of the spiritual process is about becoming more in touch with those aspects of the Frontal Lobe's functions (ironically much of which is stored in the Left half of the Frontal Lobe!) However, one of the other major functions of the Frontal Lobe of our brains is the ability to "keep in mind" images and sensations from the past and "recreate" them in whole or in part for inspection. This little "movie theater" in our heads gave us the ability to conceptualize reality and overlay the natural environment with a "memory" or even an artificial mental construct and hold it in mind regardless of what the external world is showing us. In short, it is one of the primary tools that allows us to live outside of what the world offers us in the present moment. As a tool, it's been a powerful ally in our survival to date, as a way to live life however it's exactly as if we were living our lives through a television character on our favorite show (the show called "me"), rather than what we perceive in the "real" world. And God help us if that little show in our head turns from say a light comedy, to a family drama, to a horror movie that now holds us hostage in a painful reality that we can no longer distinguish from the reality of our present existence. The development of the Frontal Lobe of our brains is one of the primary reasons why we are able, for the most part, to live almost completely "in our heads" in an image of our own construction.

And so it can be seen that the Frontal Lobe of our brains is both a blessing and a curse. In fact when discussing hemispherical dominance, the left half of the Frontal Lobe (the distinction between left and right is more symbolic in nature because both hemispheres function in most all human perceptions, we're discussing dominant perception vehicles, - e.g. which half is playing the biggest role in the processes, not absolute locations) is an important player in the role of bringing peace and joy in our lives. Combined with how the Right Hemisphere (in general) perceives reality, the Left Prefrontal Cortex helps in the generation of feelings of joy, happiness and compassion (as suggested by the work of Dr. Richard Davidson.) And so, in fact, both hemispheres play a part in how we feel joy and happiness in our lives, but one half (the Left) tends to bring with it many many pitfalls that can hold us in a spell of our own self created pain. And when we live in the self created images that we play out in our frontal lobe movie theaters, it can become a torture chamber if that creation is conditioned to be a painful or bleak view.

Two Hemispheres of our Brain

"There are two aspects; one is conceptual, dynamic consciousness which is full of concepts, and the other is transcendent consciousness. Even the concept 'I am' is not there. Conceptual, qualitative Brahman, the one that is full of concepts and is qualitative, is the outcome of the functioning body. This consciousness is dead to me; it is gone. I have transcended that. So, whatever is, is that other consciousness, that one which is without concepts."

- Nisargadatta Mahajaraj

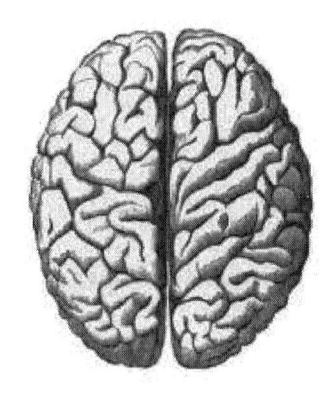

I'd like to begin the discussion on the two hemispheres of the brain with a little parable that I wrote, I will let it speak for itself before continuing:

The Two Sages

A young Seeker of the truth travelled across many miles to the foot of a mountain where two sages lived that held the mysteries of the universe. As he approached the foot of the mountain he saw a simple structure made of wood. It was basically a wooden floor with four beams holding a wooden roof above it. Standing in front of the two sages who both sat cross-legged, one in complete silence and the other chanting softly to himself, was a small boy.

As the Seeker approached the small boy spoke "Who is it that approaches the Sages of Enlightenment?"

The Seeker stopped in his tracks and responded "I am Joe Lostsoul, I am here to speak to the great sages and learn the truth of reality."

The boy cocked his head then replied "I didn't ask your name Seeker, I asked who you are."

To this the Seeker was at a loss. After some thought he then proposed, "I am a man from San Jose, California and a citizen of the United States of America."

"I didn't ask your sex or where you lived Seeker, I asked who you are." responded the boy boredly.

"I am a software engineer and I wish to consult the sages."

"I didn't ask your profession Seeker, I asked who you are."

The Seeker paused and considered his response and the boy sat patiently waiting. Finally after much consideration the Seeker replied "I am the son of my parents Lilly and Jacob Lostsoul."

"I didn't ask your lineage Seeker, I asked who you are." the boy's demeanor didn't alter in the slightest nor was his tone angry or jeering. It was factual and calm. The Seeker was again at a loss. The boy sat patiently with a very compelling smile on his face. He seemed quite disinterested in whether or not the Seeker was going to speak further. The Seeker was running out of things to suggest and stood silent for a moment before the boy. After a long while in silence the boy finally spoke:

"You're getting closer Seeker..."

The Seeker had no idea what the boy was referring to and this only added to his confusion. What answer did the boy need to hear? The Seeker could think of no other way to describe who he was to the boy. He felt a deep need to speak to the sages but could not solve this riddle that barred his entrance. The boy sat patiently waiting but the Seeker was out of ideas.

"I'm afraid I do not know the answer to that question" the Seeker finally said in resignation.

"Then you may enter" replied the boy and who then stepped aside.

The Seeker was confused but didn't want to wait around for the boy to change his mind and so moved quickly past the boy and approached the sages. The sage on the left was rocking slightly back and forth and mumbling to himself while the sage on the right sat completely still and silent. The Seeker was beyond excitement in anticipation of finally receiving the truth. He fell to his knees before the sages and prostrated himself before them.

"Oh great Sages of Enlightenment, I have come seeking the truth! What is the truth of the universe and who am I in it?"

The sage on the left answered immediately "You are the greatest soul ever to reside in a body."

The sage on the right remained silent.

The Seeker responded "Oh wise Left Sage, I don't understand does that mean that all other souls are less than I am?"

"Nothing in this universe is greater than you are. You are the center from which all the universe spins. You are the hub of the wheel. Nothing of any importance happens that does not relate to you" continued the Left Sage. The Right Sage again remained silent.

"But how can this be, I will die one day and I will no longer exist!"

"When you die the universe dies with you. Without you there is nothing." replied the Left Sage.

"I don't understand, did the universe exist before me?"

"No before you, there was nothing. No one." the Left Sage continued.

"How can that be? What about my parents?"

"Your parents exist to create you, without you they have no existence." replied the Left Sage.

"That doesn't make any sense to me. How can that be?"

"You are the center of the universe, nothing exists without you."

The Seeker was baffled by the Left Sage and looked over to the Right Sage who sat quietly and motionlessly. In his eyes was a depth and calmness and a hint of compassion and the Seeker was quite calmed by the gaze of the Right Sage. The Left Sage went back to mumbling to himself while the Seeker took in all he had heard. After a moment the Seeker finally turned to the Left Sage:

"So, when I die the entire universe dies with me?"

"Yes, it is yours take what you will from it. All belongs to you" replied the Left Sage who immediately went back to mumbling to himself under his breath.

"So I can take anything I want at any time?"

"Anything that you desire, take it it is yours."

"But how can I do that?"

"You reach out and grasp it. Do what is needed. Take what is yours."

"Anything!?"

"Anything." the Left Sage went back to mumbling to himself.

"But what happens when it is consumed or if it no longer satisfies me?"

"Then find something else to satisfy you and take it instead."

"But what if other people try to stop me from taking it?"

"Then they are wrong and they should be punished. Devise a way to punish them and implement it."

"That doesn't seem fair."

"Anything you do in that cause will be right and just."

This seemed odd and the Seeker turned to the Right Sage whose gaze was constant and compelling but who remained silent.

"But what if they fight back?"

"Then bring greater force than they are able to and overcome their resistance."

"What if I am unable to do so?"

"Then you will be a failure and you will diminish. And if you go, so does the entire universe. You don't want that do you?"

"No, no I don't."

"Then do as I say Seeker" concluded the Left Sage with great forcefulness and confidence. The Seeker stood and absorbed what was said. The Left Sage went back to his mumbling. The Seeker felt emboldened and ready to seek confrontation in a world of potential competitors who might wish to take what was rightfully his. He turned and began to leave when an idea hit him and his feeling of greatness dwindled immediately.

He turned back to the Left Sage "Wait, how can this be true!? There had to be a universe before me and there must be one after I am gone!"

"No, there was nothing before you and nothing will remain after you are gone."

"That makes no logical sense."

"It is true and that is all you need know" replied the Left Sage who went back to his mumbling.

The Seeker remained unsatisfied and turned to the Right Sage who gazed up at him with a depth in his eyes and a kindness in his smile.

"Do you have nothing to say on this subject?"

The Right Sage was silent and remained motionless but quite alert.

"You have nothing you can offer me in my pursuit of truth?"

"That one says nothing, ignore him, he knows nothing of the truth" mumbled the Left Sage who then continued, "Go and do as I say."

The Seeker remained unconvinced and gazed at the Right Sage.

"I know you know something, what can you show me?"

"All he knows is what he sees, hears, feels, smells, tastes, and touches in this present moment. He has no wisdom of what is important. Go and listen only to me and return with all that your heart desires" demanded the Left Sage.

The Seeker hesitated. Something inside him knew that the Right Sage had something for him. The Right Sage made no motion toward him nor movement of any kind but held his gaze with a look of love and compassion. The look alone was enough to make the Seeker calm and without need for a brief moment.
    "Don't fall for that parlor trick, it's just a fleeting feeling. Go and take what is yours!" demanded the Left Sage slowly becoming angry. "Do you not have the common sense to take what is yours!?" he continued and his anger was rising to fury as he continued, "WHAT KIND OF FOOL ARE YOU!? DO YOU WISH TO BE A NOBODY!? A NOTHING!?"
    Just then the Right Sage offered his hand.
    "Don't take that it's one of his parlor tricks. Hocus pocus, it's not real" warned the Left Sage.
    The Seeker looked into the eyes of the Right Sage and saw a peaceful and calm gaze staring back at him. Trust filled him implicitly and he found he had no reason not to reach out and take the hand offered by the Right Sage. The instant their hands made contact boundaries of his body vanished and he could no longer define the boundaries of his skin and body as opposed to the energy that surrounded him. His consciousness expanded to fill the space which had no apparent bounds. He knew, without thoughts and without words, by direct experience that he was one with all things and that individual things were in fact an illusion and that there was no difference between the energy that made up his body and the energy that made up everything around him. He felt peace and harmony vibrate throughout his body which had expanded to become the entire space around him. He looked down and his human body looked small and insignificant and he felt that there was no way he could squeeze himself back into that little vessel. Moreover, he knew he didn't want to. Why would anyone chose to feel small and insignificant when the truth was just the opposite? He had found universal truth and it came from listening to the lies of the Left Sage and experiencing firsthand the truth of the Right Sage. The comparison between the two states allowed him to perceive reality in a way he never thought possible. He had reached Enlightenment.
    In this parable the Left Sage and the Right Sage are in fact representations of the consciousness of the Left and Right Hemispheres of the brain. In the search for the answers to the question of the mystery of

the "self" the two hemispheres are quite different in their approaches. The Left Hemisphere is always ready to offer hypotheses and theories about who you are, and always with itself as the center of importance. The Right Hemisphere however, existing outside of the realm of language and time, is silent but constant and when listened to will offer you the experience of the entire universe as yourself. The Middle Way, that the Buddha talked about many years ago, comes from feeling both perceptions simultaneously. Enlightenment is the process of sensing through the Right Hemisphere as the primary perception focal point, whereas we seem to be naturally inclined to do so through the Left and because of how the Left Hemisphere perceives the universe, it makes one feel small and constantly "at war" with the environment. Peace and ease come from the serenity of the Right Hemisphere which knows by direct experience that it is one with all things and that the universe and itself are inseparable.

Why We Need Two Perceptions

One of the primary reasons why we need two perceptions is because we fall into two evolutionary roles and those are as predator and as prey.

When we are predators, we need to objectify the universe. We need to bias our own form over others and seek out other forms to "prey upon" or steal energy from to gather it to our own form. If we saw everything as "us" we would be very hampered in this biological need and so we need to "switch" to a perception of the world where there are adversarial "others" that may or may not serve as a food source for our further survival. Our Left Hemisphere provides us in this endeavor with a sense of separation from the world and an ability to see images as individual objects so that we can "pick out" details of high interest for us to decide whether or not to pursue as food.

However once satiated we switch to a "safety in numbers" prey animal approach to survival where many pairs of eyes increase our survival rate by spotting potential predators and then alarming the rest of the group of their approaches. In such an environment a perception of a group "us" is needed that includes a very empathic structure for bonding. And so, it is clear that there must be a part of our perception that sees the company of others as a pleasant situational experience, or we simply would not seek out such environments. Our Right Hemispheres help us out in this by allowing us the ability to meld with a group consciousness, or rather to let go of a single sense of "me" in place of a much wider sense of "us," and this comes from the Right Hemisphere's perception that no longer feels like an isolated form in a sea of other forms.

How Our Hemispheres Perceive

"(Each hemisphere is) indeed a conscious system in its own right, perceiving, thinking, remembering, reasoning, willing, and emoting, all at a characteristically human level, and . . . both the left and the Right Hemisphere may be conscious simultaneously in different, even in mutually conflicting, mental experiences that run along in parallel."

—Roger Sperry

The very top of our brains is a layer of mass called the "Cerebral Cortex" (which also includes a frontal portion called the "Frontal Lobe" which has already been mentioned) and it is split into two distinct "hemispheres." This is the portion of our brains that separates us from the bulk of the rest of the animal world, and it's often nicknamed "The Monkey Brain" as opposed to the lower level of the brain the "Limbic System" that is often nicknamed the "Reptilian Brain." Each hemisphere contains a portion of the Cerebral Cortex and the Limbic System, but as it turns out the predominant "view" of the universe through each of our hemispheres is quite a different show. We will now take a moment here and familiarize ourselves with the two "halves" of our brain and the very different views of the universe they project. It is important to remember that unless your hemispheres are disconnected by severing the Corpus Callosum (which is the part of the brain that links them in communication and function) they both function simultaneously at all times and in virtually all human behaviors and perceptions. When "Hemispherical Shifts" are discusses this is more in terms of which of the hemispheres we allow to be the "dominant" view. And, depending on which one is in "control of the ship" we experience two distinctly different "rides" in this little vehicle called "The Human Body."

The Left Hemisphere

"Thinking, or more precisely identification with thinking, gives rise to and maintains the ego, which, in our Western society in particular, is out of control. It believes it is real and tries hard to maintain its supremacy. Negative states of mind, such as anger, resentment, fear, envy, and jealousy, are products of the ego."

-Eckhart Tolle

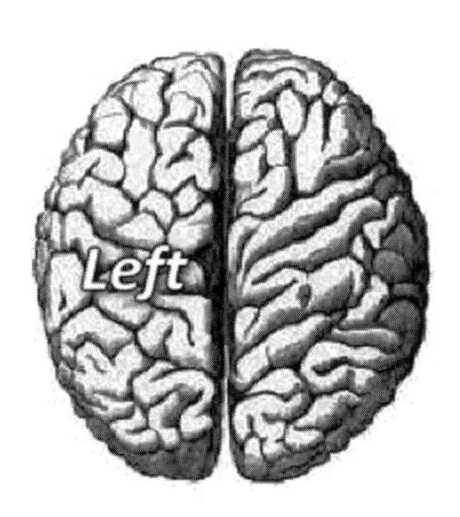

There is a calculation device of unparalleled ability that is half of your brain. Here are some of its functions:

- Language: word definitions, sentence structure, storytelling, internal "brain chatter", and memory recall for spoken or written messages
- Detailed analysis of information (evaluation functions - giving data a "positive" or "negative" value, future and past cataloguing - timelines and orders of operation, creating ideas and "facts," and linear reasoning)
- Controls the right side of the body
- Numerical computation (exact calculation, numerical comparison, estimation)
- Forms strategies based on current evaluation functions of known (previously experienced) material
- Defines the limits of our bodies (generates a feeling of being separate from its environment)

Though often vilified in spiritual texts, the functions of the Left Hemisphere are a great reason why we have come to be the most dominant species on the planet. They are NOT the enemy. When used correctly they can be an amazing tool for the manipulation of the external world and for the solving of finite (limited number variations) problems (like language and mathematics, etc.) that can be used as illustrative tools to create a world of our choosing. However we have warped that tool and begun to use it for a purpose it was not intended. We are now, due to the demands of our artificial world, expecting that the Left Hemisphere create an "artificial self" and maintain it through beliefs and certainties that it draws from personal experience. And this was NEVER nature's intended usage for our Left Hemispheres. And, while it does "the best it can" to fulfill that purpose, due to its narrow beam of focus, when it is in charge of "piloting the ship" it tends to "bump into things" and cause pain and suffering, or in the words of Albert Einstein:

"The intuitive mind is a sacred gift and the rational mind is a faithful servant. We have created a society that honors the servant and has forgotten the gift."

So, with that in mind I'd like to go over some of the functions of the Left Hemisphere and how they are often used to generate a "false self" and the painful limitations generated by the beliefs or more tragically certainties created in that process.

Evaluation Functions

*"In the absence of my Left Hemisphere's negative judgment,
I perceived myself as perfect, whole, and beautiful just the way I was."*

- Dr. Jill Bolte Taylor

The Left Hemisphere of our brains has only one of two evaluations to give incoming stimuli and that is either positive or negative. The evaluation of zero, or no evaluation, or "simply as it is" is not an evaluation it is capable of assigning because it needs to catalogue the conclusion about the stimulus into useful "beliefs" that it can use to navigate future situations of a similar nature. The evaluation of "nothing" gives it "nothing" to build upon, so, it will work very hard to lean an evaluation toward one of a positive or negative nature even if it has to craft a story around the event that doesn't exactly fit with the facts as actually perceived (more about this phenomenon in "The Story Teller" section later.) Due to this necessity it tends to over dramatize events so that it can stretch it into a clearly positive or negative assessment. Once it has achieved that goal it will then place the experience into the overall "Story Of Me" that is narrated in our heads by our Left Hemisphere Language Centers and the event is added with either a "bad" or "good" evaluation and then the Story Teller function of the brain weaves "important bits of detail" around the event and places it in the timeline of "our story" before moving on to the next evaluation. Some appraisals of experiences contain a fairly insignificant value and don't get to play a large "role" in the "Story Of Me" while others are abstracted as highly significant and become major "plot elements" in our stories. And it doesn't really take much introspection to see which ones those are; they are the ones we tell (or hear) over and over either out loud or internally in the form of our "brain chatter," or from the voices of those in our lives. Needless to say, these stories hold special significance and very high evaluations of either positive or negative and shape the way in which people make the choices in their daily lives.

    We then tend to scan our present experiences for events or objects that we "expect" to see and abstract from the selective view "significant" details that reinforce beliefs we already hold. If we do that long enough, we will turn the "belief" into a "certainty," and that certainty is a cage and a limit to who we are and what we are capable of in this life. When these certainties are painful (like "I am not good enough" or "I am less than others" or "everyone is always cruel to me" etc.) they hold us captive in a very painful prison and cause great amounts of pain and suffering.

I would now like to share an essay I wrote about this subject matter and I hope it speaks to you:

Problem Solving, The Barrier Between You and Peace

There is a standard misconception that grows with age that we have gotten as far as we have by the repetitive "solving" of "problems." As we look back on our lives we trust the Story Teller's (a language based Left Hemisphere brain function) version of reality that we came upon a "problem" that we then, through examination, strategies, and thinking overcame and moved forward. This, however, when examined doesn't hold with facts, and in seeing this clearly we can break free from the painful certainty that this world view holds us under.

Brain cells are funny little creatures that wire brain functions together based on where we place our awareness in the moment. The more we focus our awareness on certain kinds of things, the more those brain functions get placed on a list of "high priority functions" (otherwise known as "conditioning.") These high priority functions, in time, become so over stimulated that they no longer need EXTERNAL sources to fire. In fact, when there are no external sources the brain supplies INTERNAL sources (by conjuring mental situations where these high priority functions would be used - e.g. anxious story telling about possible future "problems" or fantasizing about future situations where this or that behavior will be the "solution" to the fantasy, etc. or by ruminating past events and replaying them over and over to see where a different behavior would have "solved" the problem etc.) and the purpose of this is to keep the system "stimulated" so it can retain its high priority status. And this, over time, can become a trap, a very painful trap that causes us to try to escape FROM OUR OWN MINDS through denial mechanisms and practices that take us away from "ourselves" like drugs, entertainment, etc. Of course, all denial mechanisms are of a temporary nature and these unresolved issues keep coming back again and again, strengthened by the fear that they will fall from high priority status through lack of use. And the cycle continues...

But when we examine our lives with a cold and rational view we see that the majority of the problems that have come and gone in our lives were not solved by strategies, but by time which distanced our attachments to certain people, places, and things and that emotional and intellectual distance allowed our brains to "let go" of the problems with no strategies whatsoever. In fact, if we were candidly honest about the REAL story of our lives we would see that it was VERY rare that the strategies we devised to "solve" the problems ever did more than create more and more suffering while the painful event was unfolding in terms of self generated pain by resisting what was happening and wanting it "not to be." The struggle generated by creating strategies to avoid what is, is in fact what the Buddha referred to as "Dukkha" when describing the human condition. And it's a very painful way to live...

And because we believe the "Story Version" of our lives we more and more get to a place where we trust "no one but ourselves" and our own "problem solving" abilities as the means to avoid pain (present and future.) And in that trap it is only the surrendering to the fact that this perception is painfully inaccurate that allows us a chance of freedom from its clutches. And as a pointer to this my teacher used to say to me often "So, Mark, how is that working for you??" Of course the part of my brain that wanted to keep my "problem solving" as a high priority function would be quite threatened by such questions and want to avoid contact with the people who would ask them to keep "safe" the mental functions that I had, through repetition, placed on high priority. In short, I avoided him for long periods of time when he asked me such powerful and important questions. And IF such a clear question feels threatening to you use that as a wonderful pointer!! What REAL thing can be threatened by a question?

So how do we get out of the addictive trap of perpetual problem solving? By Accepting what Is, fully. Because, if you accept something as it is fully, you take away the "problem" status assigned by the brain. Now, of course, the problem solving portion of the brain will do everything in its power to trip up this practice because it is a threat to its status as a high priority function and so will try to turn "Accepting what is" into a "problem."

"I just can't seem to accept what is!? I don't know what I should do differently to figure out how to accept what is! I need to think about this and solve this problem... etc. etc. etc."

Well, when that occurs, it's time to accept again, NOW accept that you can't accept! Keep the problem solver out of the entire process and it will slowly but surely fade as you retrain your brain to see "problem solving" no longer as the front line defense mechanism to perceived reality.

It takes time to do this, and it can only be done as a practice in the present moment. But, fear not, each time you accept what is fully, you send a new message to your brain that peace in the present moment is more important to you than problem solving, and slowly but surely your brain re-wires for peace. Don't become discouraged, that's just a way for the brain to try to de-rail you by placing a negative evaluation on your practice (all positive and negative evaluations are Left Hemisphere functions and attempts to maintain control of the ship...)

So, in the end, where's the problem? It's only in your mind. The present moment can only bring what is, and the solution to challenges in the present will usually have quite obvious and very simple, non strategically based answers (hungry? find food... etc.) And when it's an emotional problem, accepting your attachment fully is an important step out. Just broke up with a loved one? Well, were they worth the pain? All things end, to have them now, you must pay later when they're gone. Were the good moments worth the bad? I think when you look with a grateful eye at your life you will see they mostly balance out and we didn't show enough gratitude when things were going well to keep us through the times when the downward swings in life took us away from what we were clinging to. Again, not a problem, just an unavoidable pattern of life that is solved by the natural turns of the "Wheel of Samsara" (Samsara is a Sanskrit word meaning "continuous movement" or "continuous flowing" and, in Buddhism, refers to the cycle of birth and death and the constant flow of change in the universe).

So, let go of problem solving, it hasn't been the boon of escaping your problems that your brain has sold you. In fact, it's the primary cause of suffering in everyday life, in the form of creating mental problems for this process to "solve" when no external source is available. It doesn't serve you. Let it go. Accept what is, and take the problem solving functions of your brain out of the game and out of your daily life where they create far more suffering than they ever prevent. And when there is a genuine problem that needs a strategic solution, you will naturally begin the process, no perpetual practice needed. The problem solver is a great tool, but when you make it your life, it makes your life into a problem.

Symbolic Language

"For that which can be spoken is not the eternal Tao"

- Lao Tzu

Now that we've got this Frontal Lobe to hold images in our heads, how do we communicate those images to others? Well, we'll need to assign symbolic sound patterns to the external world and agree that when I say the word "cat" I'm indicating the same thing you are. That way, when I think of a:

I can then turn to you and say "cat" and you and I will have an indication of what I'm thinking of. Without the ability to hold images in our minds, it's not really necessary to go through all the trouble of building an entire language when I can just point to a:

which will have to be within range of our senses in the present moment, and "grunt" an indication to you to notice it. No further need will arise in the communication for me to get you to understand that I am indicating the animal. From this simple illustration we can see that the development of the Frontal Lobe of our brains necessitated a specific skill set so that we could communicate what we saw in our mental movie theaters to others. From this need came the development of Symbolic Language, or sounds (symbols) representing something outside of the sound itself. And what a wonderful invention it was. It can be said with little fear of contradiction that the development of language was primary in Man's rise to the top of the food chain and the domination of the planet. But, is the word "cat" really the same as the actual animal? It doesn't take much to see that the symbolic sound pattern "cat" is not the same as the creature itself. And yet, how often do we embrace the truth of this in our lives? When our children ask us questions like:

"How come when I pull my wagon with a ball in it, the ball rolls to the back of the wagon?"

And when we reply:

"It's inertia Johnny..."

Do we really think we've taught Johnny something concrete about the universe that he's become a member of? All we have done is describe a label, a symbol of the process that is inertia, and not the process of inertia itself. Well, that's fairly easy to see with a process, but it's not as easy to see, though still true, with a cat, an idea, or a person. Just because we can assign a label to something does not mean we know what it is, or even that we've experienced it as it is. And yet, any label that our Language Center decides to conjure to describe a thought, object, or any perceived event we accept whole heartedly and rarely, if we are honest with ourselves, do we question if the label gives us anywhere close to a real indication of what it is we're labeling. And then, along with the label, our Left Hemisphere assigns an evaluation of +/- to it and stores it for future reference. We then move on, confident that we know what it is, and what its value is relative to the rest of the universe. Of course, all such estimations must come from a data pool of our previous experiences, and so it's easy to see that if we got it wrong the first time, all future evaluations will carry the same flaw building upon it like a house of cards until reality decides to show us where the flaw in our belief lies by bringing reality to our doorstep in a way that we can no longer deny that our evaluation was painfully inaccurate. And it all begins with the process of assigning a symbol to it and trusting that the symbol is an accurate representation of what it is. Language is a tool for communication, but we often forget that and lean too heavily on it to generate our worldviews and beliefs.

It has often been said of words that they are mere "pointers" pointing or indicating something else, and the something else is what is important, not the pointer itself. In the Zen tradition this is often described as:

"Mistaking the finger pointing at the moon for the moon itself."

Or another metaphor often used in spiritual language is:

"Mistaking the sign post, for the destination it points toward."

In that light I would like to offer a short spiritual observation that I wrote some time back:

Let Go of Pointers

What concept can a tiny human brain conjure that encompasses an infinite and omnipresent universe's (or being's) existence or intentions? All concepts, the moment they are formed are terribly over simplified and ultimately meaningless when talking about the universe as a whole, or God. Words, concepts, methods, pointers, are all only useful if they send you toward a personal state where you, by dropping them, embrace God in this moment as God presents this moment to you. Arguing about methods, pointers, words, phrases, ideologies and beliefs will be a very painful path in this process. If nothing that a human brain can conjure in the way of a concept can hold God, then the only way to embrace God is by letting go of concepts and embracing what God is giving you Now. What mistake is God capable of making? Why would you toss away the gift of this present moment? You don't like or agree with what God is giving you now? And you have come to this belief how exactly? I think, with a simple "looking" at this, you will see the clear downfalls. No word or method or pointer is "the truth" not even the excellent pointers: "the now," "Awareness," "consciousness," "Atman," "Christ or Buddha nature," "Samadhi" or even "perfect." Embrace God by letting go of concepts and when you do your nose will smell God. Your hands will feel God.   Your ears will hear God. Your mouth will taste God and your eyes will see God.   And in that silent embrace you and God are one.

Time Sense

*"To be identified with your mind is to be trapped in time:
the compulsion to live almost exclusively through memory
and anticipation. Time isn't precious at all, because it is an illusion.
What you perceive as precious is not time but the one point
that is out of time: the Now. That is precious indeed.
The more you are focused on time — past and future — the more
you miss the Now, the most precious thing there is."*

- Eckhart Tolle

(combining two quotes from "The Power of Now")

If there were no Frontal Lobe to hold memories and/or fantasy projections, there would be no need for the concept of time. Life would be perceived as it actually occurs, and that is as one long stream of the present moment. However, along with the formation of thoughts and language came a need to catalogue those images and the "timeline" was invented. Did I see the "cat" before or after I saw the "river" and so on.

The timeline is a mesmerizing invention and quite powerful at bending our worldviews to its demands. Not many people ever come to the realization that time is a completely conceptual thing. It does not exist. Time is a relative comparison between "now moments" that we've catalogued in our brains. There is no actual "past" or "future" because we can only experience those concepts in the form of memories or fantasy projections in the present moment. We watch our movies about the past and projections about the future in our Frontal Lobe Movie Theater but we can only do so NOW. Time is a purely conceptual device that we use to organize bits of stored memory in a sequence. It's not real. A clock is a device that changes numbers in a predictable pattern, it does not keep track of "time." Humans set specific clocks as the "official clocks" and all other "clocks" then conform to those official clocks and we then agree that it represents "time." In fact the mechanical clock was an invention of monks as a kind of "alarm clock" so that they would know when it was the right point during the day to perform their daily prayers. It's an entirely human created construct, an agreement to abide by rules of behavior, NOT an actual thing existing independently in the universe. No Frontal Lobe, no time. A tree is a living creature that will outlast many a human being, and yet, to a tree, the question of "what time is it?" would be an absurd question. The answer the tree would give, if it could speak would be "What are you talking about!?"

The notion of time however is so engrained in our worldview that while we are able to see this if we stretch ourselves and even nod in agreement, the moment this is done we fall back under its spell and go back to the world of the past and future. Why? Because the half of our brain that is currently piloting the ship has no purpose in the present moment. It MUST catalogue thoughts that occur in the present into evaluations and stories, and it's always working JUST behind the curve. Once the perception comes into our brains, it's fixed and final. And it's that, very recent past, that the Left Hemisphere has to deal with. The present is "untouchable" or "ungraspable" to it and so is meaningless to it. It's threatened by it, because it serves no function there, and prefers to live in the past or daydream about the future.

You are here, even if you dream of travelling to distant lands, the one thing you can never actually achieve in these dreams is not actually being here. Let go of the need to constantly look ahead or behind and be here now. It's where you always are, why resist that truth by constantly looking away?

So, in conclusion, let me restate that: time=change. All we can do is compare this now moment to other now moments and note the changes. The changes create the illusion of time. It's very similar to making a flip book animation. If you change the location of the little stick figure he "runs" across the page. Our brains notice the change, and create a "timeline" that remembers the sequence of the changes. Timelines are just a mental construction. There is only the now.

I cannot recommend highly enough Eckhart Tolle's "The Power of Now" for a further inspection of this subject matter. And when you read it, remember, it's always the right time in your life and that time is always, now.

The Ego

"For what I am seems so fleeting and intangible, but what I was is fixed and final. It is the firm basis for predictions of what I will be in the future, and so it comes about that I am more closely identified with what no longer exists than with what actually is. It is important to recognize that the memories and past events which make up a man's historical identity are no more than a selection. From the actual infinitude of events and experiences some have been picked out – abstracted – as significant, and this significance has of course been determined by conventional standards. For the very nature of conventional knowledge is that it is a system of abstractions."

-Alan Watts

There is a sensation that comes from the Posterior Parietal Gyrus (a section of our brains in the Left Hemisphere) otherwise known as our "orientation association area" that we are a single separate structure from the energy that surrounds us. And without this brain function, we would feel, which is closer to what we really are, no distinction between "us" and the energy that surrounds "us." However, without the distinction that we are a separate entity from the rest of the energy of the universe we would be unable to bias this form (our body) and "protect it" from harm. In other words, if we held the same value for the energy that makes up our body as the rest of the universe holds (that it's nothing "special") then we would not continue to work so hard at preserving it. So, from a strictly evolutionary view, it's easy to see that having a view that biases the perceiving form over other forms would be very useful, if not essential for a species to continue. However, as it turns out, there are really only a few times during our day when this bias is of primary importance and the rest of the time it's only important to have access to it if the need arises. When we need to eat, for instance, it's important for us to bias our form over the form we're consuming, as well as if something or someone is threatening to harm us, it's important to have circuitry that biases our form over the harmful form to protect the integrity of our bodies, etc. However, when there is no imminent threat, this need is lessoned substantially, and in fact the perpetual sense of being "on guard" is a very stress inducing state and can lead to many health issues and much suffering. And yet, it is where we tend, in modern society, to spend a substantial amount of our waking hours (and many of our sleeping hours) and much of this behavior is completely unnecessary and ultimately harmful.

    The feeling of separation is closely linked to the functions of the Amygdala (a part of the Limbic System of the brain) which has the function of interpreting incoming stimuli to see if it merits the fear or rage response (often called the "fight or flight" response.) The more separate we feel from our environment the more likely this portion of our brain (and it gets the first crack at all incoming stimuli) has of firing and invoking a response (in order for us to fear or rage against something, it certainly has to be seen as an "other.") This state of constant "readiness" causes much stress and suffering and can be linked to many diseases and health issues. Let alone the fact that it's just an unpleasant way to experience the universe in this human form.

Along with this feeling of separateness comes the ideas and beliefs that we have abstracted from our past experiences that we have clung to as "our own." Eckhart Tolle often calls this process "investing thoughts with a sense of self" and that is an excellent way of describing the process by which we choose our beliefs and behaviors. It is very rare that people ever examine their beliefs or behaviors until they cause them great pain or suffering and so often times it's the only time they do any "work" on themselves and their energy levels are depleted by the suffering from the circumstances in their lives. This makes for very slow going, as when the "Wheel of Samsara" turns and their "luck changes" they very often abandon the practice and go back to life on "auto pilot" until reality again forces them to examine their beliefs and so on and on until they die still clutching their unexamined beliefs. This can lead to a dismal existence, or stated more directly to quote Socrates:

"The unexamined life is not worth living."

On the surface this quote can be seen as an aloof statement that those who do not examine their lives are somehow inferior to those who do, but that is not how the quote is meant at all. Socrates is pointing out here that if we move about the world without examining the processes that drive our thoughts and behaviors we are then prisoners of what those thoughts and behaviors bring into our lives. And, why would someone choose to live at the mercy of the beliefs and behaviors that were handed to them by their environments and families when through simple observation of those thoughts and behaviors they can take control of their own lives and live in a manner of their own choosing? Socrates sees the act of not choosing one's own life as a life not worth living. And I can't agree more with his assertion. However, in order to do this effectively it is important that we view the beliefs and behaviors from an objective space, and that takes practice, as well as learning how to access that space in this complex perception tool that is the human brain.

As it turns out the part of our brain which can give us a perception of the world free from pre-determined evaluations of "positive or negative" is the view offered to us through the Right Hemisphere of our brains. Its primary job is to give you the view of the present moment, right here, right now and within that perception it feels completely at ease and even joyful and full of wonder. From this perspective the various issues that our Left Hemisphere takes "seriously" or "fears" naturally seem silly and meaningless. All of our beliefs and behaviors viewed from this vantage point slowly become more stable and less "serious" and "fearful" having as a resultant residue a feeling of greater peace and joy in our daily lives. But it takes some time to "get used" to viewing the world through this lens and so in the beginning there are many ways that our Left Hemisphere trips us up and even tries to fool us that it's a part of the process.

In the end, the thoughts that flow through our heads are not us, nor are they of our choosing, they are products of where we have in the past placed our awareness. And like consumers in an open market, we can, by not engaging (or in consumer terms "buying into") them, lessen their strength and the rate at which they occur. Conversely where we choose to focus our awareness we strengthen those bonds, and like consumers in an open market, we "vote with our dollars" by "buying" the products we prefer, or in the case of or our minds by focusing our awareness on peaceful and blissful circuits we increase the amount that those processes appear in our perceptions and thought processes.

But this all begins with noticing that we have an ego in the first place. That we have a sense of separation from the rest of the universe and beliefs and behaviors that we cling to through investing them with a sense of self. Most people suffer from Socrates' "unexamined life" and never get the chance of living in a manner of their own choosing. And ask yourself this simple question:

Who, given the choice, would choose to suffer or cause suffering in others?

So, from this, it is clear that only the unexamined mind is capable of causing suffering in our lives and the world at large.

The Story Teller

"As my left brain language centers recovered and became functional again, I spent a lot of time observing how my storyteller would draw conclusions based upon minimal information. For the longest time I found these antics of my storyteller to be rather comical. At least until I realized that my left mind full-heartedly expected the rest of my brain to believe the stories it was making up! Throughout this resurrection of my left mind's character and skills, it has been extremely important that I retain the understanding that my left brain is doing the best job it can with the information it has to work with. I need to remember, however, that there are enormous gaps between what I know and what I think I know. I learned that I need to be very wary of my storyteller's potential for stirring up drama and trauma."

- Dr. Jill Bolte Taylor from "My Stroke of Insight"

The language centers of our Left Hemisphere are a very chatty bunch. The portion of our brains that generates speech (primarily, though not exclusively, this is generated in a section of the brain called Broca's Area located in the front half of the Left Hemisphere) chats incessantly with the portion of our brain that understands speech (primarily, though not exclusively, this is generated in a section of the brain called Wernicke's Area located in the latter half of the Left Hemisphere of the brain.) This internal brain chatter is made up of bits and details, and though some are seemingly random bits of data that just "pop up" throughout our day others string together into little "stories" that we store for future recall. The portion of our brains that tells stories has been nicknamed "The Story Teller" and it seems quite appropriate to begin the section of the book dedicated to this function with a little story:

The Tale of the Bad Posture

A pair of middle aged married couples who had been friends for over twenty years gathered in a restaurant one evening after they attended a talk given by a spiritual teacher who had gained quite a following in the previous year due to his appearing on a very popular national television show. The first couple consisted of a man in his mid forties who made his living as a Yoga Instructor and his wife, also in her mid forties, who worked in the medical field as an x-ray technician. While the other couple consisted of a man in his early forties who made his living as a high school English teacher and his wife in her late thirties who was primarily a housewife but made some extra cash as a vocal instructor out of their home (in her youth she had attended the Juilliard School of Music and studied to be an opera singer.) They had just finished their meals and were discussing all the amazing new spiritual material they had heard when the man, the Yoga Instructor, mentioned in passing that the speaker had terrible posture. His wife, the x-ray technician, who spent many hours dealing with Osteoporosis patients immediately concurred, though they both promptly dismissed it as an unimportant detail. The other wife, the Vocal Instructor, agreed saying that she noticed it as well, and then the three turned to the English Teacher who admitted he hadn't seen that little detail during the talk. There was a brief pause, and the discussion then moved on to something else.

During the pause, the English Teacher felt like the "odd man out" and even felt a slight pang of "inferiority" because he was the only one that hadn't noticed the detail. The feeling passed and he very soon was caught back up in the thick of the conversation unaware that his mind was churning over the details of that little awkward pause below the surface.   After a few moments a thought occurred to him and he blurted out:

"You know why I didn't notice the bad posture?" and the other three people paused and turned to him as he continued "Because my uncle John was in a car accident as a young man and when I was growing up I got used to seeing that kind of thing and so I probably just subconsciously assumed he had been in an accident or something..."

There was another pause as the other three absorbed what he had said, and after some polite nodding by the other three, the four went back to what they were discussing before the interruption and the evening continued. However, subconsciously, the English teacher no longer felt like "the odd man out" and in fact felt "superior" now because he was "above" the detail that the others had found so thought provoking due to his extensive experience with such things...

THE END

And so, what really happened?
During the spiritual talk the Yoga Instructor felt very intimidated because he made his living as a spiritual instructor and felt "inferior" to the speaker's profound knowledge on the subject and so needed some way to feel "superior" to the speaker and therefore noticed his posture. The moment he did, he settled down a bit and could get back to listening because his ego felt better about the fact that the speaker

may have known more spiritual material but he was in better physical shape.

During the spiritual talk the x-ray technician noticed the posture because she feared that she was soon approaching the age where she would herself have to worry about Osteoporosis and had been taking extra calcium daily to avoid such a thing.

During the spiritual talk the vocal instructor was impressed with how clear the vocal projection was of the speaker and instinctually looked to his posture to see how well he was projecting his voice to the audience. In that process she noticed that his spine was not straight and was impressed at how little it impacted his vocal performance and even for a moment began to doubt the great Swedish and Italian masters who proclaimed that such a thing was of primary importance to projecting one's voice.

During the spiritual talk the English teacher was very conscious of how important it was to listen to the speaker because as someone who made his living speaking to a classroom of students who rarely recalled what he had said the day before, he knew that focusing on the words of the speaker was very important if he wanted to recall what was said in the talk later at the dinner table with the others.

So, in reality, the English Teacher simply hadn't noticed the bad posture of the speaker because of the multitude of details that were possible to notice in the evening his perception had not picked out - abstracted - the detail as significant. So why at dinner did his brain concoct the story about his uncle to explain how he HAD noticed and then dismissed the detail? Well, there is a part of our brain that will "re-write" reality into a story that better fits our needs or expectations. It draws from the past and then, based on what it expects to see in situations similar to the one it's perceiving (either in the present moment or in a memory played out in our Frontal Lobe Movie Theaters) it simply adds detail where such detail does not exist to fill in the gaps that we are unable to notice in the moment. Of course, all the details it adds are ones that conform with what we'd LIKE those details to be, or what we expect them to be. Through this process we move about the world in a very selective personal show seeing only what we expect to see over and over until we convince ourselves that only what we expect to see actually exists.

The upside of the Story Teller function of the brain is that it's excellent at projecting "what-if" scenarios about what we've experienced and running them over and over in our minds so that we can derive expectations about what we might experience in the future. It's a wonderful tool in that regard and is responsible for many useful functions of human thought, but it doesn't have a predilection for what TYPE of story it runs, and it's just as satisfied running stories about potentially joyful scenarios as potentially terrifying ones. It also, sadly, has no predilection for fact over fiction. In fact, it seems to much more prefer fictitious details that fit into expected outcomes than real details that force it to view the universe in a new or different way. Due to this fact it is therefore even more important that we examine the beliefs and certainties we have gathered over the years that determine our expectations. Otherwise, if we have generated a very bleak view of the world, our Story Teller will insure that all its works of narrative fiction fit into that view and the caliber of our daily lives will become torturous indeed. Another quote from Dr. Taylor might illustrate this point more clearly:

> *"I wholeheartedly believe that 99.999 percent of the cells in my brain and body want me to be happy, healthy, and successful. A tiny portion of the storyteller, however, does not seem to be unconditionally attached to my joy, and is excellent at exploring thought patterns that have the potential to really derail my feeling of inner peace. This group of cells has been called many things; some of my favorites include the Peanut Gallery, the Board of Directors, and the Itty Bitty Shitty Committee. These are the cells in our verbal mind that are totally resourceful in their ability to run our loops of doom and gloom. These cells tap into our negative attributes of jealousy, fear, and rage. They thrive when they are whining, complaining, and sharing with everyone about how awful everything is."*

One of the jobs of the Story Teller in our minds is to consistently re-write history to maintain the illusion that one's currently held beliefs have been consistent throughout one's life. To conveniently forget that it once held beliefs other than it currently does, thus maintaining the illusion of our "reality" as a solid unchanging entity (or Ego, if you prefer.) In this process one of the most important tales that the Story Teller loves to run is the "Story of Me" which it constantly revises to "better explain" how we currently see the universe at large.   If due to our current circumstances we have a very negative view of the universe, then our Story Teller will re-write our "Story of Me" into a tragedy, of course, if our circumstances dramatically change and the Wheel of Samsara spins and brings us an "up-swing" instead of a "down-swing" our Story Teller will revise the "Story of Me" into one that explains the new "success" of our lives as an extension of the superior way in which we've chosen to live, and so on and on as the Wheel of Samsara turns re-writing the story to accommodate the expectations that best fit the perception of the current situation of our lives.

It doesn't take much examination to see that the Story Teller can quickly turn from a wonderful ally in our lives to a private torture chamber rerunning painful stories over and over and selling them with great certainty to our minds.

Beliefs & Certainty

*"If you walk about wielding a hammer,
all your problems will look like nails."*

- Neil deGrasse Tyson

*(restatement of an older quote
but I prefer this phrasing)*

Every thought that we have is just one relative perspective of what might hold literally an infinite number of interpretations. We think it, and we believe because we've thought it we are now bound to it, it's "ours." But that simply isn't the case. Just because we think something, doesn't mean we MUST abide by it. The choice is always up to us.

There is a trick used in the training of elephants so that when they are full grown, even a creature of their size and power can be controlled and made to behave passively and tamely. When an elephant is a baby its trainers will attach it to a very firm pole to hold it in place. At first it struggles with it and attempts to escape but after a long while it gives up, unable at its infant size to budge the firmly rooted pole. Later in life, when the elephant is full grown, it is more than capable of tearing the pole from the ground with even the slightest effort, but it has conditioned itself through its repeated failure to believe that it is unable to do so and so never tries. It stands there, helpless, in a self created limitation.

In psychological terms this is called "Learned Helplessness" and it is a profoundly powerful and impactful process by which we impose limits on ourselves and believe in those limits even when the original environmental conditions that imposed those limits no longer apply. A human wrinkle in this trend is that due to the human ability to empathize and create artificial realities in our heads, humans can absorb the limitations of others onto ourselves through observation, many children inherit their parent's conditioning in this manner. In other words, we don't even need to be the person who went through the events that conditioned us to feel helpless, we can learn to see the world through that lens from observing the behavior of people who had the originating experience. Or, more plainly, the parent is traumatized into seeing the world through a negative filter, and the child learns it from observing the parent without the benefit of knowing the original source. This can create a situation where the child has no original "memory" to "get over" just the conditioning handed to them by the parent. That's a tough gift to inherit and a tougher one to overcome because there is no clear memory to show us that we are responding to an experience that "no longer is."

So, in short:

Our beliefs define our perceptions and our certainties are our limits.

If someone asked me to put what I've found into one sentence that best encapsulates what I've learned in my many years exposure to spiritual material and practice it would be the above statement. Mind you I would resist doing so, because, though many people are under the illusion that the truth must ALWAYS be simple and that the more simple the statement the more "truth" it contains, this is not always the case. I will give some examples of what I mean in two illustrations:

Simple Version:

"An eye for an eye!"

Longer and more accurate version:

"An eye for an eye making the whole world blind!"

Or, in the world of Science, even though Occam's Razor generally stated suggests:

"Simpler explanations are, other things being equal, generally more accurate than more complex ones."

We find instances like:

Simple Version:

"Black holes absorb all energy."

Longer and more accurate version:

"Black holes absorb all energy, and then, periodically some particles just 'pop out'... (A.K.A. Hawking Radiation)"

And so, even the practical belief in "simplicity" is just another limit we place on our perception. Every belief we hold and every certainty is a tremendous hindrance to our ability to look with a child's eyes upon reality as it presents itself in the present moment. And due to our selective perception we continually see - abstract - what we expect to see over and over, reinforcing the belief until it becomes rigid enough to become a certainty. And then, it becomes the limit of what we are ABLE to perceive in this universe, unless, or until such a time (which might never come) where it fails us so terribly that the pain and suffering it causes forces us to reevaluate it and we are finally able to be freed from its clutches.

If we but look at mankind's history it's not hard to see thousands upon thousands of previously held certainties that were widely prevalent in man's collective worldview that are now virtually discarded. One that is mentioned often because of how absurd it seems to the modern mind is that at one point there were virtually NO humans that believed that the Earth was anything but flat and that the Sun revolved around the flat Earth, etc. etc. etc. These two certainties, and all worldviews that were built upon them held the flaws of the foundational beliefs creating terrible limits to how the brain holding that certainty was able to view the Earth and its genuine place in the universe.

And so, it would seem evident from this that it is of great importance that we examine our beliefs and certainties and by sheer force of will hold an open mind to even that which feels the most "solid" in our worldviews. For there is a fly in the ointment. There is a fatal flaw in the process that forms beliefs and certainties and it is held in the part of our brains that generate these views (the Left Hemisphere), and that is that in order for us to believe ANYTHING we must draw upon previous experience AND the evaluation of those experiences that we assigned them in those moments. In other words, that which we have never been exposed to, to us, simply doesn't exist. Has no value in the form of a belief structure. Is intellectually invisible. And yet, to the universe has full value and function regardless of whether we believe in it or not.

And yet, how often do we REALLY question our beliefs? I think if you are very candid you will find that the majority of our day is spent in reinforcing, not in questioning our belief structures, and the older we get the more rigid we get until we find ourselves swimming in a sea of certainties that now HOLD US captive. And God help us if those certainties come with the negative evaluation that the Left Hemisphere assigns as one of two possible evaluation functions. Because that's all it has got to give you, and when you clutch onto them and "invest them with a sense of self" you empower them to BECOME YOU and run your life and your worldview for you. This process, and our blind following of it because of how persuasive the Left Hemisphere is, is what leads to what the Buddha calls "Dukkha" (loosely translated as "suffering") and is the cause of much of the pain and misery that pervades this planet.

What but certainty and beliefs would ever bring anyone to harm or kill someone over their skin color? Or religion? Or, over what artificially defined "mass of land" called a "country" they were born in? Only blind faith in beliefs and the certainties they generate would bring anyone to the point where they would act in such a way. Blind, unquestioned, un-examined beliefs that led to certainties that led to violence and hatred and fear. Or to quote one of my favorite lyricists Neil Peart:

"Quick to judge, quick to anger, slow to understand. Ignorance, prejudice, and fear walk hand in hand"

It's time to stop calculating your life, and live it.

I would like to now share an essay I wrote about the subject of certainty:

Why We Need Two Hemispheres and Certainty

We need two intelligences because we can never be certain. If one truly believed in certainty they would never move. Their Left Hemispheres, which are the source of judgment in our minds and certainty, would need to gather all the data on something and weigh it to an absolute conclusion for certainty to be real. Well, at best, the Left Hemisphere is the equivalent of drawing water from Niagra Falls one small cup at a time and hoping, in the process, to "experience the entire waterfall." Certainty is simply impossible. Luckily for the frightened and judgmental

BELIEFS & CERTAINTY

Left Hemisphere its playmate in this thing called "human consciousness" is a wily rascal who fears nothing. Who needs no certainty to act, in fact, is often reckless in the face of danger. It's impulsive, trusting, loving, and fearless, and likes to "play" in this universe that it knows through direct experience is just it. It stands by like a kid in a bathing suit waiting for the parent to check PH levels before they can go swimming, tapping its mental foot and getting tired of waiting for the Left Hemisphere to complete its calculations. The Left Hemisphere, however, never tires of these calculations and so needs its impulsive friend to, at some point, just move the body and jump into the water. Over Niagara Falls in a barrel, while, on the way down the Left Hemisphere checks the facts that it gathered from the many cups of water it analyzed and hopes to survive the fall...

In short, we simply don't have the capacity for certainty; it's a problem of space. We can't hold the amount of data needed for certainty in our little brains, sorry folks, that's what it means to take a form in the midst of the sea of formlessness, forms are uncertain, and they dissolve. That's the game we chose to play when we took on a form. So, the key is, to let go of the need for certainty, and enjoy the ride down in the barrel, because it's wonderful, even if we die when we hit the water, the ride down alone was worth the journey.

What's the Left Hemisphere for? Well, it's for increased accuracy, without certainty. An example of this can come from archery. We shoot a bow for the first time and our Right Hemisphere says:

"Wee! That's fun! Let's do that again! I like watching the arrow! Neeto!"

While the Left Hemisphere picks out details:

"Hmm, I pulled it hard and it went far."

"Hmm, I held the tip up and it went farther."
"Hmm, I pointed it directly from my body and it seemed to go straight to where I was pointing it."
etc. etc.

In time, our accuracy level rises as we make small adjustments before firing, and then, by holding the Right Hemisphere back before it makes us let go of the string, we make the adjustments first and in time we gain proficiency with the bow. It's still just "wee, look at it fly!" to the Right Hemisphere, but the Left Hemisphere begins to appreciate the progress, making a story and a timeline about it and storing it in our brain for future reference in similar activities, but never, and I mean, never reaching certainty. It's simply beyond us in a practical measurement of our interpretation of reality.

The problem is that in time, the Left Hemisphere begins to "buy its own press" and believe it has come to some certainty in areas where it has gathered a lot of data. Like if someone has given us a degree in something, or if we have practiced a method for a long period of time. We tend to puff up our chests and buy into our Left Hemisphere's stories of our "superiority" in this area and over time begin to warp our vision of reality to the exact degree to which we buy into this falsehood. The superiority we sense is relative to the human world. I, for instance, probably know more about chess than a great majority of folks who will read this essay, but that doesn't mean I know with certainty anything about the outcome of a chess game between myself and that person.

And so, when, approaching the notion of certainty, approach with extreme caution, because the degree to which you believe in it, is the degree in which you and the universe will be at odds with reality and that you will suffer from that belief.

Let go of certainty, allow your mind (Left Hemisphere) to make its "best guess" and it will function well for you and in time your "proficiency" will improve, but keep your mind open to the present moment, because the truth is, that simply anything might happen in this wonderful present moment where we all reside and cannot escape. And so, it is plain to see, to quote Dean Spanley:

"Only the closed mind is certain."

Anticipation and Reward

One of the most seductive aspects of the Left Hemisphere dominant world view is the ability of it, through checking its catalogued experiences against the present moment, to predict the outcome of events. It's been the benchmark of development for so long in our lives that we forget that it's just one of the brain's many tools and only one of the ways in which we are able to interact with our environment. Some of these processes are so automatic that they are completely unnoticed unless the anticipated event is not what is expected. In that case, if the brain is able to link the unexpected outcome to another associated experience then a joy response arises often coupled with laughter (comedians make a great living off of this phenomenon.) A simple example of this is that there are probably 100% of you that can predict what the next word is in this... ... paragraph.☺ When we get it right a little "happy" feeling comes over us (which is why puzzle solving is so popular in its many forms) and when we get it wrong, it's often no fun and we look for excuses to waylay the blame...

When we come into a new environment there is a learning curve that our brains have to go through until predictability stabilizes into a "comfort zone." Like when we acclimate to a new job, there is always a learning period at the beginning that is far more stress filled than years later when it's all second nature and nothing really surprises you any longer. Your catalogue of environmentally specific data is now so great that you are able to anticipate virtually all outcomes of experienced stimuli. In short "nothing fazes you anymore." The drawback to this is however in the words of Shakespeare that:

"There are more things in heaven and earth, Horatio, than are dreamt of in your philosophy."

In other words, we simply don't have the ability to actually go on "auto pilot" and no longer be present to what IS actually going on in our environment. In fact, it is often when people feel the most "in control" that the universe throws them the curve ball that creates the greatest havoc in their lives because they were so certain they "had it all under control" that they had simply lost touch with "what is."

The Story Teller of our brains often dismisses the times when the situations don't go as planned as irrelevant or "someone/thing else's fault" so it can maintain the certainties it has taken so long to establish. Until such a time that the experience is so painful that it can no longer maintain the fictional story and "our world's crumble around us..." Eckhart Tolle calls these "limit situations." And they are a great opportunity to reacquaint ourselves with the necessity of being present in our lives.

Of course, to avoid such turbulent and painful situations, the great spiritual masters have over the years advocated living an "Awake" life. And, simply, what this means, is no longer allowing your Left Hemisphere to convince you of its certainties and stories and every so often to "wake up" and "look about" at "what is" to verify if where you think you're steering your ship is where you actually are. And this process of "living with your eyes open" is a large part of the work of "spiritual liberation" and the rewards are a decrease in the turbulence and often deep suffering that comes from perceiving reality only from the narrow perception of anticipation and reward.

Even Christ Had To Let Go Of Beliefs

I want to remind my Christian friends that even Christ suffered from the limitations of his beliefs and certainties. For instance, Christ held the belief that he was "merely a carpenter" for many years until he finally ventured into the desert to meditate (examine his beliefs and certainties) where upon examination he was able to let go of them and embraced his divine nature. And if Christ had these limitations, what does that say about you? So, follow Christ's example and find the truth within you, or to quote him directly:

> "...the Kingdom of Heaven is within you." - Luke 17:21

Roles

*"And if a skillful human actor can take in an audience
and make people cry, think what the cosmic actor can do.
Why he can take himself in completely. He can play
so much for real that he thinks he really is.
Like you sitting in this room, you think you're really here.
Well, you've persuaded yourself that way. You've acted it
so damn well that you KNOW that this is the real world.
But you're playing it. As well, the audience and the actor as one.
Because behind the stage is the green room, off scene,
where the actors take off their masks. Do you know that the word
'person' means 'mask'? The 'persona' which is the mask worn
by actors in Greco-Roman drama, because it has a megaphone-type
mouth which throws the sound out in an open-air theater.
So the 'per'--through--'sona'--what the sound comes through--that's the
mask. How to be a real person. How to be a genuine fake.
So the 'dramatis persona' at the beginning of a play is the list of masks
that the actors will wear. And so in the course of forgetting that this
world is a drama, the word for the role, the word for the mask has come
to mean who you are genuinely. The person."*

- Alan Watts

There is a subtle shift of behavior that comes over us when the social situation merits it. We don a "social mask" and play a role knowing full well that our counterpart in the act will "improv" along with us. There is an unspoken agreement that this time, you'll play the waitperson and I'll play the customer. You'll play the boss and I'll play the employee. You'll play the politician and I'll play the mistrustful voter. You'll play the child and I'll play the parent. Or you play the husband and I'll play the wife. And, from countless hours of seeing these roles played out by our families and friends, or from viewing them on television and movie screens, or reading them in books we all know what is expected of us the moment we "put on the mask." And, then, once the mask is worn, we all "play act" accordingly.

The moment anyone steps out of the role, there is confusion, and/or even outright scorn because by refusing to play along, we jeopardize the illusion, and threaten to expose it. In some cases, the roles are so valued by society that laws are drafted to ensure that the parties play along. When the judge enters the room, we are demanded to rise. If the policeman asks us for our identification we are expected to comply. And the notion that a judge can be treated as "just another person" is viewed as a threat to the integrity of the entire system. And so it's enforced by brute force if necessary by those who see the role as too valuable to compromise. And yet, even with the law enforcing it, it's still an agreement. It's still a role. A fabrication. An illusion that is agreed upon by all players. And this truth is one that is rarely, if ever, even noticed by the people playing the roles, except, of course, when the roles are in conflict. In those moments, just for a fleeting instant of time, we get a glimpse of the illusion. My spouse and my child are arguing with each other and both are hurt. My role as spouse and my role as parent dictates that I should console them both, and yet they both look to me for the fulfillment of that role at the same time. My boss needs me at the office but my child needs me at home. My country calls upon me to service, but my family needs my presence, and so on, and so forth. And in those moments we see both roles as they are. And in those moments we choose one mask over another, however, by doing so we must first see them as masks, if only for the brief moment of choosing. We choose the child over the boss or the spouse over the child and off we go, with one feeling validated and the other feeling slighted, hurt, and betrayed, because we didn't fulfill our role obligation. We didn't play our half of the "improv" and left them hanging in the breeze. And in that moment they feel a "loss." They might not vocalize it, or even know it at a conscious level, but something was perceived as "taken" from them the moment their role was not recognized. Of course, nothing was taken. Nothing was betrayed. Because a role is merely a series of learned behaviors stored in the Left Hemisphere and played out on command when it recognizes the appropriate environment, in short it's only a concept, an illusion. And an illusion cannot be taken or given, it can only be believed or, with clear vision seen through. And when we do see through it we are free from the role. We are simply who we are.

Once we master this clear vision completely, the next time society expects us to don a mask, we can ask "is this something I need to do?" or "is this a game I choose to play?" And if we do indeed play, we will do it consciously, purposefully, knowing it's a game, with a space between us and the mask and knowing full well that the mask is not really "us."

And in that space is freedom.

The Limbic System

*"You can close your eyes to the things you do not want to see,
but you cannot close your heart to the things you do not want to feel."*

- Author Unknown

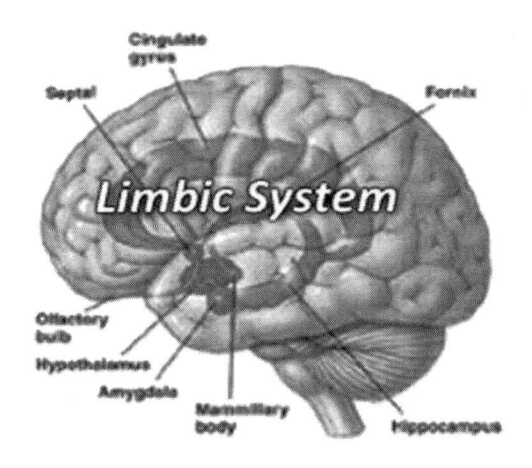

Now that we've looked at the Left Hemisphere of our brains, it's time to go beneath our Cerbral Cortex to the Limbic System as this is another cohort in the process that has the potential to make us "suffer" in our experience of the universe.

There are two primary propagation methods for species on this planet, the first is to have excellent survival mechanisms and the other is prolific breeding. Our brains are built upon the brains of our predecessors and we inherited the propagation methods that were inherent in their cognitive make up. One of the first evolutionary brains that became very adept at survival was one that evaluated incoming stimuli as dangerous or non dangerous and then once evaluated as dangerous, quickly made the second evaluation of fight or flight. Giving all incoming stimuli first crack at this evaluation increases the likelihood of survival of that species by a substantial amount. Because the entire purpose of that mechanism is the protection of the form. Constantly running away is a dangerous business because while running we might very well run from one foe that we might stand a chance of defeating in a fight into another where we stand no chance at all. Constantly fighting would mean that we will only be successful until a bigger fish comes into town. And so to have a brain function that is wired exclusively with the function of deciding whether to fear (run) or rage (fight) can be seen as a useful tool in surviving potentially dangerous environments. Our Amygdala is that function and it is one of the foundational building blocks of our Limbic System (often nicknamed the "Reptilian Brain" made up of many different systems of which the Amygdala is one) that over time became able to offer much more subtle "feelings" like envy, anticipation, remorse, respect, etc. The Limbic System has other functions to it than just the production of emotions, but for the sake of this book we are going to focus on emotions primarily, as in emotional responses we can easily become trapped and since our emotional mind gets first crack at all incoming stimuli, it can become a monster that colors our worlds with its evaluations in the form of "feelings" that keep us from an objective and more stable view of the universe. It can be argued, but for me I like Robert Plutchik's list of basic emotions which is: fear, anger, sadness, joy, disgust, trust, anticipation and surprise. He combines these basic impulses to form more complex emotional states, like the base combination of joy and trust might lead to the more subtle extensions from joy to serenity and trust to acceptance and the combination of serenity and acceptance leads to love, etc.

Once the Limbic System attaches a "feeling" to the incoming stimulus it then passes the stimulus to the upper regions of the brain for further evaluation, but it keeps the "feeling" attached to it the entire time. Once it reaches our Frontal Lobe we can try to use more "mature" or "reasoned" evaluation functions to "talk us off the ledge" and respond to the stimuli in a more rational manner. Of course, some states are easier to coax than others, fear and rage being very powerful and much harder to "steer" into a more reasonable channel.

Again, though previously stated in this book, I want to reiterate that our Limbic System forms very early in our lives (as newborns) and wires at that time due to sensory stimuli and then does not mature (or change) as the brain ages, and so each "feeling" that it generates (and what kinds it tends to generate) is not much different at the age of fifty as it was at the age of two or twenty years old. However, how often or in what context it generates these responses is a different story all together and leads us to:

Limbic Conditioning (a.k.a. Pain Body)

"As long as you are unable to access the power of the Now, every emotional pain that you experience leaves behind a residue of pain that lives on in you."

- Eckhart Tolle

Just like our beliefs and certainties, our emotional states are placed on "high priority status" (conditioned) by the focus of our awareness. When we focus our awareness on negative emotional states like fear, sadness, and anger we foster the combinations that stem from them like disgust, contempt, aggressiveness, loathing, depression, and pensiveness, etc. Telling our brains by the repeated focus of our attention that these systems are of high value and need to be kept "on alert" for easy access. And, just like the negative evaluation functions, when there is no external stimuli to run these systems, our Frontal Lobe movie theaters will run memories and fantasy scenarios to allow us to "stay in shape" or "practice" these high priority systems. Turning a wonderful survival mechanism like the Amygdala (fear/flight or rage/fight) into a torture device that colors everything we see with a horror filled sensation that leads to debilitating anxiety or a sense of contempt (a combination of rage and loathing) that ultimately leads us to a nihilistic boredom and depression. Eckhart Tolle gave this process the nickname of "The Pain Body" as a metaphorical description for how the Limbic Conditioning lies about "waiting" for stimuli so that it can come out of "hiding" and "take us over." Once it has us in its grasp, due to the fact that its wiring is the same as a two year olds, it transforms us from a fully functional adult, into a blithering, tantruming, child in the blink of an eye.

And that's no way to live.

The Right Hemisphere

"The great pleasure and feeling in my right brain is more than my left brain can find the words to tell you."

- Roger Sperry

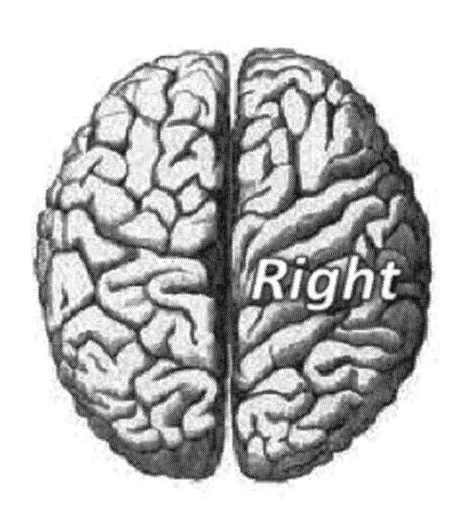

Now, we'll come back up to the Cerebral Cortex to examine the Right Half of our brains, and how this half of our perceiving vehicle experiences reality:

There is a quiet observer that looks out onto the world with the wonder of a child's eyes that is half of your brain. Its primary function is to give you your perception of the present moment. What you see, smell, hear, feel, and taste right here, right now. Here are some of its functions:

- Language: intonation/accentuation, prosody (meter of speech), tone, facial expressions, body language, contextual meaning
- Judging the position of things in space - like body position compared to the environment
- Storing in pictures and sensations past "now moments"
- Forming "big picture" collages of data, knows functions of objects instead of labels
- Controls the left side of the body
- Numerical computation (approximate calculation, numerical comparison, estimation)
- Processing of visual and audio logical stimuli (bringing you this "present moment")
- Fearless, impetuous, awe-filled, joyous

For many years the Right Hemisphere of our brains was seen as a stupid lazy lout that behaved with animal-like impulses. It was perceived as the "Mr. Hyde" to the rational and reasonable Left Hemisphere's "Dr. Jekyll." It was the beast intelligence that drove us to impulsive and emotional tirades. Oh, how wrong this view was of this peaceful, loving, and joy filled perception vehicle. And it is only relatively recently, thanks in large part to Dr. Jill Bolte Taylors "Stroke of Insight" that science is beginning to understand this marvelous and awesome tool. Of course spiritualists have been raving about it for thousands of years, but with no idea what they were pointing to, they could only describe it in metaphors and poetic language. It's time we learned who and what half of our human perception is, and find ways to tap into the peace, love, and joy that is our birthright.

I'd like to now introduce you to half of your brain. And give you some examples of how this wonderful tool functions and what gifts it brings to us every moment of our existence.

A Non Judgmental Viewing Space (Accepting What Is)

"What could be more futile, more insane, than to create inner resistance to something that already is?"

- Eckhart Tolle

The Right Hemisphere does not have evaluation functions like the Left Hemisphere because the Right Hemisphere functions in the present moment. In order for something to be evaluated comparisons must be made and those comparisons will have to be pulled from previous experience. From this we can see how the two hemisphere's complement one another, because the Right Hemisphere offers you what is, right here, right now, while the Left Hemisphere conjures what was and postulates what might be. However, since we as humans are only ever HERE, in the present moment, the only perception that is based in reality, is the one offered by the Right Hemisphere of our brain. And as such, it tends to be far more accurate a view of reality than the Left Hemisphere because it makes no errors in judgment. What you see is what you get. What it offers is what is, in this present moment and what better starting place can you be to begin a truthful and accurate journey than where you actually are? So few people take the time to fully experience the present moment and live exclusively in their heads and assign to their perception the values and judgments that they have gathered from the past. Only the Right Hemisphere is capable of accepting anything as it is, with no value judgment attached. And, so, only the Right Hemisphere is capable of seeing the universe as it is. And since it is always as it is, only the Right Hemisphere can see. See what is. See what is always true and where we are meant to be.

Therefore, when it is time to appraise who we are, and what we are, it is of the greatest importance that we begin that process by accepting what is fully and without reservation.

Without that, we are blind. We are groping in the darkness staring at figments of our imagination and hoping that they correspond to reality. And that's a painful way to navigate, it causes much pain and suffering, and yet, so few have ever opened their eyes to see what is. To be truly awake and no longer sleeping in dreams generated by their minds.

Accepting what is is the portal out of that self created trap, and the beginning of a genuine relationship with our true selves.

There is a great misconception however with the term "Accept what is" and it seems to come from a desire to attach a passive response to the end of the acceptance. The goal of this practice is to live life in accordance with the flow of the universe, what I call "effective action." And in order to do this, one must first accept what is.

This does not mean, "Accept what is, and then don't respond" there will flow from the acceptance a natural (or "Wu Wei" if you prefer - a Taoist term loosely translated as "effortless doing") response that needs no "inspection" or "thought."

And, since this action is in line with the present moment and therefore the universe, you gain the momentum of the entire universe as your ally, and your actions become powerful and take you always, where you need to be.

What could resist the force of the entire universe!?

The Present Moment

"We are all energy beings connected to the energy around us through the consciousness of our Right Hemisphere. The right brain is focused on the present moment. It thinks in pictures and learns kinesthetically through the movement of our body."

- Dr. Jill Bolte Taylor

We have a narrow focused beam in our vision called the "Fovea Centralis" or sometimes called "Foveal Vision" which is a very small, high resolution, beam that is about the size of our thumbnail at arm's distance. It's what the Left Hemisphere uses to search about the universe to find and focus upon small details. The rest of our vision is generated as a massive collage of what is. And the Right Hemisphere offers it up simply and needs no searching to find it. It needs no effort to acquire it or to swim in it gliding along like a dolphin on the crest of a wave.

When we go into our heads to view our conceptual universe, we lose contact with present moment perception and it's as if a veil was pulled over it, obscuring it, blurring it, and interrupting our connection to what is. When we lose contact with the present moment, we are, in effect groping about blindly, hoping that we navigate our environments in a safe and sane manner. But if we are honest with ourselves, we will see that the majority of our "human errors" come from losing touch with the present moment and blindly "bumping into things" while gazing at the movies in our heads. Like reading a text message while driving, we are "distracted" from reality in all its forms and so are constantly at the mercy of events that hurtle toward us that we fail to see until they are upon us and pushing us around. And then, immersed in the Buddha's "dukkha" or suffering, we look to the heavens and ask "Why!? Why did you do this to me?"

Well, as it turns out, we do the majority of this to ourselves by navigating blindly, and by accepting only our beliefs and certainties refusing to see the universe as it is, and us as we are in it. This is what the Buddha meant when he used the term "awakening" he meant being wide awake and alert to the present moment and accepting what is within it. In this space we are indeed awake, alert, alive, and accurate. To live any other way is to live in a waking "dream state" blind and groping in the dark at the mercy of the waves of reality as they thrash us about.

There is only this present moment, and so to look anywhere but here, is to be at the mercy of reality while not perceiving reality. And that's a terribly painful way to live our lives.

YOU are always here, you can be nowhere else. Merge your awareness with YOU and that is Nirvana. Abiding in the Self, Christ Nature, Buddha Nature, the Atman, or Enlightenment. That's it.

A Sense of Belonging

"The whole is more than the sum of its parts."

- Aristotle

I'd like to begin this section with a little parable I wrote about the life of a Bubble:

The Bubble's Journey

A young mother placed a pan of water onto a stove. She was about to heat the water to cook some food. She heard her child crying from the other room, so she turned on the burner and went to attend to her child.

At the bottom of the pot small air bubbles began to form. They looked about and saw one another and noticed that they were all separate forms. One of the bubbles began to grow so much that it became a complete bubble and then, suddenly, it broke off from the bottom of the pot and began to rise to the surface. As it did it looked about and knew that it was alone in this great ocean and that this journey was its and its alone. Other bubbles were also growing great enough to follow, but they were separate and their journeys had nothing to do with the original bubble's voyage. They were different, separate, not the same. As the bubble approached the top of the water it sensed that its journey was coming to an end, it began to make out a new image at the end of its journey. It feared it because it knew that when it reached the end its form would dissolve. It would lose its uniqueness, and die. As it approached the fear mounted, it tried to resist with all its might, but in vain. It finally breeched the surface and popped. Never to be seen again. The bubbles that followed were terrified by what they witnessed and dreaded the same process happening to them. They tried everything they could think of to slow the process, but nothing would avail. One by one they all followed the original bubble to the fate of popping. To the forming bubbles at the bottom of the pan this looked senseless and fearful. Why would the creator do this to them?

Above the water the bubbles merged with the air. They were embraced by the whole and knew immediately that they were never in danger and that the sense that they were separate from the other bubbles was an illusion, a trick of relative perspective. And they relaxed into the whole of the rest of the air, as a part of the whole, safe in the loving embrace of all that was always them.

The mother returned to her pot, unaware of her creation, and began to cook her meal. She felt alone in a universe full of "other" things, but she didn't want to think about such frightening things, so went about her chores...

THE END

When Dr. Taylor's stroke debilitated the Posterior Parietal Gyrus in the Left Hemisphere of her brain she lost the sensation of being a separate entity from the energy around her. She knew from firsthand experience that her separate form was an illusion of the senses, and that she was the same as the energy that surrounded her. Not all of us will get to have this experience handed to us before death, and then return to talk about it, but it doesn't take much in the form of observation to see that if EVERYTHING in the universe came from the "Big Bang" then everything in the universe is made of the source material of that "Big Bang" which was energy. Lots and lots of energy. And that energy has made a long fourteen billion year path, with billions and billions of collisions and mergings and formings, to ultimately become you. You were meant to be. You are an extension of the Big Bang. YOU are simply an expression of it, and an inalterable component of the process that it began. Every seven years or so a large portion of your cells (pretty much everything except the DNA) is replaced by new matter and the old matter is gone and its journey is no longer tied to your form. The cells that resist this change, however, are predominantly in the cerebral cortex of the human brain. This is the portion of our brain that stores our experiences and evaluations and memories. However, the bulk of your form is really only about 7 to 10 years old at most. So that means that the largest portion of what was once you, is no longer you. It seamlessly went back into the "Big Bang" energy and went along its merry way. And you didn't notice a thing, because the transfer of energy "outside" your body into energy that is "now you" is constantly happening. To the universe, the "you" and "not you" are one in the same. Half of your brain knows this through direct experience and the only thing that can convince you otherwise are thoughts, concepts, and the perception of separateness that your brain generates so that you are able to bias your form in order to survive. But, it's just a trick of the senses. It's an illusion. A phantom.

To the Left Hemisphere of your brain this concept is quite frightening, because many of its functions begin with the perception of itself as a separate object. How can one evaluate anything, without separating the "parts?" However, it's easy to forget that it's just a mental construct, an imposed conceptual overlay of reality as it is, and not reality as it truly is.

Luckily for us, half of our brain is completely at ease in this more accurate perception. The Right Hemisphere of our brains knows from firsthand experience that it is one with everything around it and enjoys the safe "embrace" it feels when it gazes about at that which is merely just more of itself. Having no artificial limits placed on its perception of the universe, it feels expansive and loved and nurtured as part of the whole. And it is no coincidence that when Dr. Andrew Newberg and Dr. Eugene D'aquili monitored the brain activity of Tibetan Monks and Franciscan Nuns they found that when the people meditating reported they were in the greatest state of peace and bliss that they had found a great decrease in activity in the Posterior Parietal Gyrus. That the feeling of "separateness" was lessened by a reduction in blood flow. It's no coincidence because as they turned off this illusion generation device, and felt their natural state, they knew from firsthand experience that they were one with all that is. And so, of course, are you.

Joy and Wonder

*"We are shaped by our thoughts; we become what we think.
When the mind is pure, joy follows like a shadow that never leaves."*

- Gautama Buddha

There are many animals in the world that spend a great amount of time just sitting still. They rest, and do no perceivable thing. On the surface it would seem that they are simply abiding in themselves - being - nothing more. As a human we might want to project upon them some kind of mental gymnastics, like they're sitting thinking deep thoughts, but that anthropomorphic (the projection of human characteristics on non human objects) view is more than likely not even close to what is going on inside the animal. The animal, not being motivated by any external need, sits and rests and does little else.

    We share much of the same brains with these creatures and so, asking why the animal behaved in that manner does seem to be a useful question. Preserving energy is of primary importance but it's too cerebral a reason for why the animal does what it does. Rest, in general, is pleasurable, without that feeling of pleasure the animal would shun the activity unless forced to out of fatigue. As it turns out, when one is completely at rest, with nothing going on in the mind, a powerful bliss comes over us that is impossible to describe without feeling it firsthand. I was first able to access this peaceful wiring in my brain after much time practicing "inner body meditation" and in doing so, engaging my Right Hemisphere enough that the Left Hemisphere chatter and constant evaluations slowed greatly. Emerging from beneath the chatter and the mental noise was this deep deep peace and bliss. It's the most amazing sensation I've ever felt and I tap into it many times during my day now that I have complete access to it. But, why is it there at all!? At first, I was happy to have access to it, but it didn't make any sense that it was there at all, and then, one day, I was watching my cat and KNEW that he was also doing what I was doing. His eyes were not closed, but also not focused. He was at ease and not on alert. And he was not DOING anything, just sitting. In fact, when he noticed I was looking at him it was as if for the first time I could see that he noticed too that he and I were in the same space. Now, obviously, this could be a projection of my mind, but the sensation was pretty powerfully real to me. Not that my cat was "talking to me" but that he and I were "in the same space" if you will. I'd love to wire us both to an fMRI and see what's going on there, but suffice it to say, in that moment it dawned on me why there would be a pleasurable sensation in just sitting still. It would seem to me that in an animal that is both predator and prey (and this housecat falls into that category even though he's more wired as a predatorial animal his size would classify him as really both predator and prey) stillness would be an evolutionary survival mechanism because most predators eyes have very strong motion sensors. Mind you, this is MY personal hypothesis and I've never tried to prove it, but it makes sense to me that any creature that might be the prey of another animal would stand a much better chance of survival by either moving quickly (constantly even in the case of some fish, though this brings much attention to them) or by sitting very still. And, the inducement to sitting still seems to be that when we are completely still, both physically and mentally, a strong pleasurable sensation comes over us, and the reward for the behavior keeps us in the behavior.

However, no matter what the reason, when we quiet the chatter in our Left Hemisphere, and find a way to access the Right Hemisphere we gain access to some amazingly peaceful and joy-filled wiring that is impossible to explain without personal experience. Suffice it to say, in many spiritual disciplines there are great warnings about becoming a "bliss-junkie" and just sitting in this blissful peace day after day while doing nothing, no-thing. In fact, when Eckhart Tolle had his major shift in perception, he sat on a park bench for years and just "blissed out." Of course, not having any formal training, no one was around to warn him about that kind of thing, but in the end, he came out of it himself and went on to help others. I remember wondering why ANYONE would go to a cave and just sit and stare at the wall alone like so many aesthetics have done in the past, but now, having access to this peaceful wiring, I often wonder now why more people don't. Of course, the answer is, that most people can no longer feel it through the constant chatter and mental machinations of their Left Hemisphere.

Another byproduct of the connection to Right Hemispherical wiring is a sense of wonder. The Right Hemisphere's domain is the present moment, and anything that is able to process the present moment must be completely open to newness. Since the Right Hemisphere is not preoccupied with the extraction and evaluation of details, it needn't have a "reaction" to what is other than complete acceptance. And the emotional feeling that accompanies the complete acceptance of new stimuli is wonder. Simple, and joy-filled wonder.

Why do we begin to lose our wonder as we grow older? Because our certainties become hardened and locked into personal evaluations, and we train ourselves more and more to filter the world through our Left Hemispherical perception until, in time, we are no longer able to just sit and marvel at how amazing existence in ANY form is. The fact that there is anything as opposed to nothing is simply amazing and when we are able to let go of our thoughts and certainties and just gaze about our child's eyes re-open and we again see and feel this awesome universe from the heart. It's beautiful, incredible, and non threatening because in that space we feel firsthand that it is just an expansion of that which is us.

Left Prefrontal Cortex

As it turns out part of our Left Hemisphere would seem to play a part in this feeling, I would say it's where the feeling is modified and amplified (that's my personal experience and seems to correspond to how the Frontal Lobe works, as an amplifier or modifier of existing sensations, like a volume knob that increases or decreases the feeling of bliss, but I digress, and will leave this to the professionals to figure out...) Dr. Richard Davidson, using both EEG and fMRI scans, studied Tibetan Monks during deep meditation and found very high activity in the prefrontal cortex - especially on the left side (which has to do with feelings of joy, happiness and compassion, ironically the right side seems to be the volume knob for negative emotions, which flip-flops the "spiritually significant" locations of these functions in the Prefontal Cortex, seemingly monitoring the opposite side's world views!? Who know for sure, only the future of neuroscience will map this more clearly, remember left and right are more symbolic representations of brain functions than actual locations) The EEG recordings during deep meditation showed extremely powerful Gamma waves in that area of the brain.

Now in a bizarre personal note, when I personally access my "feeling of bliss" I retrace the sensation of the first time I felt it rush through my brain, and the pathway was from the frontal left side of my brain, backward and then over to the right half of my brain... I used to call it "back and to the right" in my brain, I have no idea if I was sensing the pathways or just using it as a sense memory technique, but when I read about this I was not shocked to read about the peace being generated from the left frontal lobe of the brain.

In closing let me say, that our feelings of Joy and Bliss are completely WITHIN US and no external source is needed to tap into them, nor provoke them, and no external source is able to take them from us (possibly even death!) The liberation that is often spoken of in terms of "enlightenment" is primarily of this nature, that we are completely free of external sources for our internal peace and bliss. We've just forgotten for the most part how to access this wiring, but it's far past time for us as a species to remember how and quite possibly the survival of the species might very well depend on how well we succeed in this task.

Fearlessness and Adventuresome Spirit

"Praise the virtues of fearlessness. A truly fearless person embraces even death without any kind of hesitation."

- Atharva Veda

There is a curious little rascal that is half of our brains and it LOVES newness, and embraces novel experiences. It's the twinkle in all of our eyes. It's the part of us that say "Oh, to hell with it!" and dives right in. And every time it does our Left Hemisphere screams "No!! Wait!! We haven't thought this through yet! We need more time to consider this or that or did you EVEN LOOK AT this other thing!?" Of course by that time, it's too late, we're over the cliff and LOVING the ride down. We hit the water, there's a big splash, a rush of aliveness, and then, as we're swimming to the embankment the voice returns - Debbie Downer:

"Well, that wasn't too smart. You could have killed us. Way to go..." and on and on it goes.

Did you ever wonder what that dialogue in your head is all about? Who is exactly chastising who!? Well, it's the Left Hemisphere barking at the Right Hemisphere, but it's important to remember, just because our fearless friend doesn't have a loud voice (it has a quiet and calm voice that often comes in the form of just one word, or no word just an impulse, but I digress...) doesn't mean it has to be bullied about by the blowhard Left Hemisphere.

So, more directly, The Right Hemisphere is more involved in processing novel situations, while the Left Hemisphere is mostly involved when routine or well rehearsed processing is called for and in order for the Right Hemisphere to flourish in new environments it has to have a fearless and wonder-filled perception of new situations. And it does, oh, boy, does it!

Non Clinging Sense of Love

*"In love there is always duality, opposition between partners.
But in compassion the two beings are one. Love is relative.
Compassion is total communion between two beings.
But without wisdom love is blind."*

- Taisen Deshimaru

When Christ first felt the sensation that lead to his response:

> **And the second is like it: 'Love your neighbor as yourself'**
> **—Matthew 22:39**

It came from his new found connection to the perception through his Right Hemisphere. The Right Hemisphere doesn't see the universe as a bunch of "other objects" but feels naturally that it is looking at an extension of itself. When it does make out energy that could be seen as a "person," it knows directly, without being told to as a "rule of behavior," that it loves it fully. And this is NOT the object filled, clingy, possessive love of the Left Hemisphere that is the subject matter of many thousands and thousands of movies and books, this is a feeling of universal love and when the Buddha felt it he decided that he needed a different word so that it wouldn't be confused with "romantic love" and so used the term "compassion." Taisen Deshimaru's quote above is his attempt at describing the difference between "romantic love" and the love felt by the Right Hemisphere. And EVERYONE has access to this, however, over time, by filtering our perceptions more and more through the separating filter of the Left Hemisphere we slowly begin to feel more and more isolated. And, in time, we start to sense other people as "strangers" or even "potentially dangerous." Forgetting a time when we were kids where who we were going to spend the day with was whomever was sitting in the sandbox when we showed up to play. Well, that wiring isn't gone forever, it's just been weakened through a lack of use. And it's past time we got it back, not just for our sanity, but for the sake of the human race as a whole.

I'd like to now share with you a piece I wrote about love, I hope it speaks to you:

Simple Reflection

What would you change about something you loved completely? It's clear upon simple reflection, that if you loved something completely, you would change nothing. Therefore, love is the acceptance of someone/thing exactly as it is. And, since no so called "inanimate object" rejects anything else in the universe in the least, (name something a rock rejects?) it's clear upon simple reflection that love binds the universe. Since, God, (as stated in every religion) is "omnipresent" or "everywhere at once" then upon simple reflection we can see that God is love. And, since we, are all, merely parts of the whole of the universe (our bodies were forged in stars) then again upon simple reflection we see that we are God. And if we are God, it is clear upon simple reflection, that we are love.

Intuitive Sense of "Knowing"

"If the single man plants himself indomitably on his instincts, and there abide, the huge world will come round to him."

- Ralph Waldo Emerson

Here is normal, garden variety, Left Hemisphere mental functioning:

A situation arises and a choice must be made. Immediately we know what we are going to do. Then, we engage our problem solver to solve the "problem," which is merely the problem of which justification we should use to do what we are going to do anyway. After a short while, when we dream up the correct justification for why we should do it, we do it. And then, we wash, rinse, repeat each time adding the extra steps so that we convince our evaluation functions that we are choosing the "right" path instead of the "wrong" path. After years of this we convince ourselves that we "think through" our choices in life and without the "thinking" we would make errors and be in danger, etc.

In contrast to this, however:

There is a little voice inside of us that comes as an impulse, and won't elaborate further. It comes to us as a clear "urge" and we "know" without thinking where it is guiding us. Afterward, of course, the Left Hemisphere's Language Centers can "sell us" against its suggestion, and it is in those times that people will often say:

"My heart is saying one thing, and my head is saying another..."

And what they're talking about is that their two Hemispheres are in conflict over the evaluation of the current experience. Now, before we continue this further, I want to say, that there are times when we "see phantoms" where we intuit ghosts that aren't really there. It does happen, it just happens far more rarely than the Left Hemisphere wants us to believe. In fact, I'd say that it happens so rarely that in a statistical analysis of the phenomenon it can be said to be "statistically insignificant." And the intuitive response to the stimuli was "close enough" and only needed to be guided by further information or adjusted with new stimuli which the brain had not yet experienced. And then it rights its course all by itself. But that's not the Story the Left Hemisphere wants to sell us and when we make small errors of perception, it wants to highlight them and run a story about them that is similar to:

"See! You are walking around blind! If you had only thought that through more carefully that wouldn't have happened to you! Now, let ME guide you and this will NEVER happen!"

And over time, we buy this sales pitch. In fact, the older we are, the more we buy it and the more we fall prey to trying to "think everything through" and since thinking can only come from evaluations of previous experiences, more and more, through this process, we become wired into the certainties and beliefs we already possess, until we can't see anything else in the world. And we know where that leads...

What if you accepted that mistakes happen? What if you accepted that we're never going to get it "perfect?" What if we see that our mistakes have shown us far more in terms of useful material than the so called "successes" of our lives? What if we embraced mistakes as lessons we were meant to learn in the first place? Then, knowing that, we can go back to piloting the ship the way it was meant to be, from a simple space of looking at what is, and responding intuitively. Or, just "knowing" where to go. Trusting that the intuitive response is the right response, even when it makes mistakes. Trusting, in the words of poet Robert Graves that:

"Intuition is the supra-logic that cuts out all the routine processes of thought and leaps straight from the problem to the answer."

And since, the launching point for intuition is the present moment, and you can be nowhere else, it must be where you were meant to be, so trusting that voice takes you where you are meant to go. Along the way, you will learn the lessons you were meant to learn. When logical problems present themselves, bring out the calculator (The Left Hemisphere) and solve them, then put it away and move on.

And you're always where you're meant to be, doing what you're meant to do. Abiding in who and what you are. How could that be wrong? What could be more meant for you than what actually occurs in your life? Or, to quote Marcus Aurelius:

"Accept whatever comes to you woven in the pattern of your destiny, for what could more aptly fit your needs?"

Common Left Hemisphere Strategies to Maintain Conditioning

"Ego is basically the movement of the mind toward objects of perception in the form of grasping and away from objects in the form of aversion. This fundamentally is all the ego is."

- Adyashanti

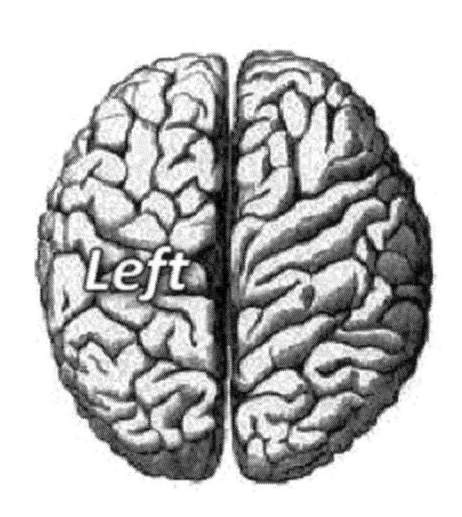

What Does The Ego Want?

What does the ego want?
A greater ego to hold as an authority.
Someone to "tell it like it is"
A larger ego with great certainty
And a never ending supply of energy
To prove it to the lesser souls.

What do egos need?
Someone to look up to
And others to scowl upon
A group to call their own
And a truth to hold dear

What do egos fear?
The possibility that there are no groups
The idea that there is no truth
The knowledge that we are all one
And the possibility that they don't exist

Anywhere But Here

The Left Hemisphere is in control of the ship and the fact that you are reading this book through its language centers is enough to warn it that there is mutiny afoot. And it doesn't like that at all. In fact, if at many times during your reading of this book it didn't try to sabotage you, or to distract you away from this book already I'd be pretty shocked. You see, it takes this stuff VERY seriously. In fact, the ONE thing that can be said about the Left Hemisphere is that it takes EVERYTHING very seriously. TOO seriously. It's a very serious little man/woman in your head, and it doesn't like all this talk about "Right Hemispheres" and "all this love nonsense!"

And it has your best interest in mind. At least it thinks it does, it has the very best intentions, no doubt it does, and to quote Eckhart Tolle:

> *"...but that's where the proverb - the phrase - comes from 'the road to hell is paved with good intentions' this is where the ego (the Left Hemisphere) says 'I want to protect myself and I need the best for myself, of course...' Wonderful intentions - it always creates havoc, not only in people's personal lives, but collectively, the ego, the collective human ego creates even worse havoc in the collective which you can read about, when you read a history book..."*

So, this very serious and purposeful energy is not going to hand over the reins to an irresponsible, silly little nit wit. How's the work going to be done!? Who's going to take care of all the problems we have!? Who...?

Now ask it:

"Who generated the problems in the first place?"

And listen to the crickets, because that's all you'll hear from the Left Hemisphere, until after a moment it regains composure and brings out its blame list:

My parents
My spouse
The government
My kids
My boss

Those damn (...fill in the blank with opposing political party or religious groups or...)

Hoping, desperately hoping, that it keeps your awareness focused:

ANYWHERE BUT HERE

Because that's the Left Hemisphere's primary deception, it's a mental "sleight of hand," a magic trick to take your attention, your awareness, away from the source of the bulk of the pain and suffering in your life, and that's that nagging, never satisfied, voice in our heads that says that this moment, this wonderful moment where we actually live, is not enough. And it's amazingly effective at this, because it only has to deflect your attention for one small pulse of a moment to make you miss EVERYTHING that ACTUALLY is. And it's a master at this, constantly making you chase the phantom of the future that is always just out of reach, just around the corner, HURRY you might miss it!! Go! Run! Faster! Faster! What are you sitting around for!? Are you lazy? Go! Go! Go! Happiness is just over there! Go get it! What are you waiting for!?

And we run about like a house pet tricked into chasing the red dot from a laser pointer, constantly leaping from place to place, looking ANYWHERE but at the source of the laser beam. And it's time to get off the ride. It's time to exit the Wheel of Samsara and leave our Dukkha behind. But the powers that be, in our brains anyway, aren't going to give up without a fight, and there are many many tricks in its bag to keep you looking:

Anywhere But Here

And here are a few of its favorites. This is not a comprehensive list, because remember, it knows you better than you know yourself, it IS half of your brain, so it's clever enough to keep changing, but the goal will

ALWAYS be the same, to keep you looking away.   We'll begin with one of the most common:

"Yeah, yeah, I've already heard this before..."

This is the front line of defense for the Left Hemisphere. If it can convince you that the subject is just something to "understand" and "categorize" and "evaluate" and "store for future use" like some product that you already possess, then it hopes from this to convince you that you needn't do anything more with the subject. You already "own" it. Of course, the subtle truth that it hopes you don't see with this process is that "understanding it" isn't the same as "living it." Don't let your Left Hemisphere "Yeah yeah" your peace away. It doesn't have the answers, if it was enough to just "understand it" then ask it where the peace and bliss is? It already "knows" this stuff why do we need to look at it anymore, well, next time you think this thought, ask yourself how this "method" has worked for you in the past? If just "understanding" a concept were enough, then you should already be at peace...

If you're not, then don't listen to "yeah yeah..."

Spirituality IS practice. Not understanding.

We can understand that smoking is harmful all we want, but until we quit smoking, what use is the understanding?

What's the Point?

When we approach this material for the first time all we have to compare it to is what we've experienced in the past. And, since this material, if practiced in earnest, will take you to a perception that you've never fully experienced, all such comparisons will be inadequate to give you a clear picture of what the result of the practice will be. I don't wish to get too outside of people's comfort zones, but as an illustration I can't think of any more clear/or accurate example than trying to describe what a sexual climax feels like to someone who's never felt one firsthand. Would they believe it with mere words? Would words do it any justice?

Well, similarly, this has to be experienced to be understood. If the Left Hemisphere tries to convince you that it's just a process that will get you "more of the same" it couldn't be more wrong. Or if it tries to compare the freedom and bliss you will ultimately experience to anything it HAS experienced, EVEN the aforementioned sexual experience, it will be wrong. It is an experience one needs to feel firsthand to understand, and so only by doing the work will we be able to choose consciously which state we would like as our baseline perception.

And, I know of no one personally who has experienced the bliss of complete liberation who has asked for their old conditioning back.

Not one person. That alone should tell you something.

Do the work, and don't let the old conditioning sell you otherwise.

Fighting the Fire While Feeding the Flame

One of the most insidious techniques the Left Hemisphere has for keeping you from doing the work is by convincing you that you need to gather more material on the subject matter before you "settle down and practice." The logic runs:

"Ok, now I know that the Left Hemisphere keeps me blinded to reality by constantly demanding more and more details for it to categorize and evaluate and make beliefs from and that that process makes me blind to the present moment and therefore to what actually is. Ok, I accept that, NOW, what I need to do is find more books about this subject matter to gather more data on the subject and get a really good idea of what it is... etc. etc. etc."

I call this "Left Hemisphere Hijacking" or, the process by which the Left Hemisphere convinces us that IT is "just here to help" and that it played a big role in getting here now it wants to "stick around" and be of service. When I think of this I'm reminded of all the movies where the murderer "helped" the police department look for the "real killer" etc. In the guise of "just being helpful" of course, but in reality they were looking to sabotage and hijack the process...

Don't fall for this! This is one of the primary reasons why people fail to do the work! The work IS practice and the practice is in NOT doing mental gymnastics. Don't fight the fire, while feeding the flame!

Seeking Salvation in Time

Since the Left Hemisphere can only function in timelines and stories it is constantly trying to convince you that your happiness lies in those functions. Either by creating wants, which is looking to the future to supply happiness in your life, or by reminiscing, which is looking to the past for happiness in the present moment. And neither of these brain functions ever quite fulfill their promises. Reminiscing about the past is never quite the same in the present because we can never fully convince ourselves that the past IS the present. We can fantasize all we want, but the one thing we can't do is actually GO BACK to the past. Of course, the Story Teller has warped what actually happened in the past pruning out any possible factors that might taint the memory and over time making it more and more "golden" but we don't mind that because when we want to use that memory to escape, it helps if it's more "pure" than what really happened. If everyone associated with the golden memory was golden as well, perfect little people who acted perfectly in a perfect past situation, then when we fantasize about it we hope that it will give us the happiness we hope to get from the activity all the more powerfully. Of course, when we're done reminiscing, our evaluation functions make the present moment pale by comparison, and the suffering continues until we find a way back to our fantasy version of "me" and so on and so forth. Well, since we can never actually recreate the past in the present it is obvious with very little inspection (living Socrates' "examined life") how this is a failed strategy for happiness in the present moment, which is the only moment we will ever exist within. Wants, or more directly "hoping that a future event will make me happy" holds the same paradox in that it's never the future and so as we live our lives constantly looking to the future to make us happy we miss the fact that that is also a failed strategy. We will never live in the future, and so, like a donkey with a carrot dangling from a stick before it, we keep walking forward hoping to "catch up" with the prize on the end of the stick, which is always "just out of reach." For those of us that actually "get the prize" it doesn't take long before we find that the prize wasn't what we thought it would be and we need a new carrot to follow toward the future "happiness" and the insanity continues. And we never stop to ask if the processes work. We keep buying it when our Left Hemisphere sells us the next bag of goods because THIS time it really will work! No! I promise! You didn't do it right! Try it this way! And so on, and so forth, perpetually dissatisfied and unfulfilled, as it keeps you looking anywhere but where you actually are.

It's time to get off the ride. It's time to ignore the carrot on the stick, because it will NEVER fulfill its promise of happiness in the present moment.

But, it's true...

The rich are dominating the poor. The politicians are bending the truth. There are people starving in the world. Somewhere, there is an injustice being committed. And every word of it is true. Your Left Hemisphere wants you to analyze it. It wants you to see it as a problem and to catalogue, judge, and tell stories about it. It wants you to ruminate and stress over it. And, added to it, it carries the extra weight that it's all true. And every time you focus on these truths your Left Hemisphere feeds on oxygen rich blood and the synaptic connections in that section of your brain strengthen and gain more ground. They maintain their high priority status and dominate your world view. Wait, you say, but it's true!

Here is my question to you:

Why is it more true than you?

Why is your existence any less true than any of these problems you are spending your precious time ruminating over? Does any of your stress over these issues change the issues? Or, does it just feed the problem solving portion of your brain? You know the one, the one that when there is no external source to feed upon, turns YOU into a problem to solve! Yeah, that one. So, again, I ask you:

Why are any of these issues more important than your peace? Isn't your peace also part of this universe? Isn't it also true? Why are these issues more important than you?

Accept what is, and release it from you. Allow it fully, and let it go. The one and only thing you know for certain in this existence is that you are. You are far more true than any concept. Honor that, and let go of stressing over things you have no control over. In the end it has nothing to do with the issue and everything to do with stimulating the over fed Left Hemisphere of your brain.

Don't get fooled by "But... It's true!"

So are you.

Specialness

As we've already discussed the Left Hemisphere contains within it the perception of separateness. A feeling that there is a "me" in a sea of "others." And, within that sense of me, in order to "stand out from the crowd" our Left Hemisphere loves to feel "special." This is an assigning of a "positive evaluation" on our perception of our individual/separate form. And, it's the "green light" for the bulk of our rationalizations that keep us in our Left Hemisphere conditioning.

"I've had a bad day, worse than most people's, so I need a drink..."

"They've never had it as bad as I have so I have the right to be angry..."

"If they had to live through what I've lived through, they would feel bad too..."

"I've never fit into that crowd, therefore what they think or feel doesn't apply to me, and so I dislike them..."

But what is the basic structure of all of these kinds of mental impulses? They are all woven on the following structure:

> "I'm suffering, and no one cares, therefore I have a unique problem that deserves a special solution..."

And what is that solution? Well it depends upon what parts of your brain have been so over fed and over stimulated that they need excessive amounts of blood to maintain their structures. If it's the "problem solver" which is quite common, then it will use the "specialness" rationalization as a way to feed.

"I am special in my misery, in fact, I'm more miserable than other people, this is a problem that needs to be ruminated over..."

And, blood flows... Without the "specialness" the gravity of it wouldn't be as powerful, and the amount of blood it needs (due to being grossly over fed) would be less. This is why there are some people who just "need drama" in their lives over and over. Drama (of course it doesn't help that it is fueled by a culture that watches approximately 7+ hours of television/media a day) is defined in screenwriting terms (I know this as I was one) as "conflict." Conflict creates a "me" and some "adversary" and a "problem" to solve. What a great way to feed those parts of the brain that torture us daily. Then, when we feel the terrible mental states that are generated from such behaviors we conveniently look externally for the source. "They did that to me!" or "What he did to me..." "She did to me..." etc. When, in reality, the source was all within. It was inside of our brains in the form of the "problem solver" and the "story teller" (which generates the rationalizations that give the "green light" to feed) and the "evaluation functions" that assign a "negative evaluation" to the situation, etc. etc. etc. and they all work in a symbiotic neural net to get access to that oxygen rich blood which keeps them over fed and dominating your world view. And the choice is ultimately yours. No one else can make the choice. YOU have to place peace and joy above these states and when they come calling, it's up to YOU to say "no thank you" and push them away from the dinner table. If you do not. If you fall prey to their machinations then you will get more of the same. It's that simple. We are all a part of the same energy stew that pops up and creates little "forms" which then dance about for awhile before falling back into the energy only to one day come out to play some more. Let go of "specialness" and just be. What have you got to lose except your misery?

Warping "Accept What Is"

Ok you've decided that there is great truth in the practice of "accepting what is" and you begin to apply it in your life. Remember, as you do this, that the Left Hemisphere of the brain needs to give perceived impulses an evaluation of either positive or negative. It simply can't function with an evaluation of zero, or rather with the evaluation that that which it perceives is merely what it is. Only the Right Hemisphere of the brain can hold up an image of the present moment as it is without judgment. So, the way that the Left Hemisphere sabotages the perception of "Accept What Is" is by subtly warping it into either "aloof indifference" (a feeling of being superior to the sensation) or "resignation" (a feeling of being inferior to the sensation) and both of these states are NOT Accepting What Is. Watch for this subtle warping of perception and when you are able to distinguish between the differences in all three perceptions (superior, inferior, and just as it is) you will be well on your way to liberation from all evaluation functions and the painful certainties that will ultimately be created from their continued reinforcement.

Chasing Past Spiritual Experiences

After much practice and study, we have a "breakthrough" and we sense the infinite. Our thoughts quiet substantially and we feel one with "everything." Bliss and peace flood our bodies and we are here now, fully. It's magical. It feels like "not us" because we've conditioned ourselves to believe in the "high priority systems" that have been experienced in the past, and we've already labeled THAT as "us." So, THIS can't be us! It's a "mystical state" or a "state of meditation" or "trance" it's anything but "us." We're that never satisfied, always looking around for more sensation, not THIS! And so, after convincing ourselves of that, we switch back to the old wiring and listen as our Story Teller begins to weave a story about "what external sources caused that 'not me' sensation." Once we buy into the story, we then sit and think about it, "wishing" to "get it back." We sit and "recreate" the external sources hoping that the magic moment "pops back up" and we can "experience that state that isn't us" again. And it's all hogwash.

There is no experience that you can have in this body that isn't a "human" experience. It was you. It's just a perception that you don't use that often. In fact, since it was the perception of the here and now, and you can't be anywhere else, it can be argued quite profoundly that it is more you than the "you" you currently identify with through habitual conditioned experience.

Drop the story about "how you got there" and you'll be there. It's the story that's stopping you. Let go of stories, evaluations, thoughts, beliefs, and certainties, and you're there.

Now, don't go back. It takes courage, and at first it takes great effort, but in time you "get used to it" and you can hold it as your natural state.

The "Ah-ha" Trap

There is a similar phenomenon that occurs with what is often termed as "Ah-ha!" moments. This is that feeling of bliss that comes when pieces to an intellectual or philosophical puzzle finally fit after much struggle with the concept. And it feels WONDERFUL. Freeing. Liberating. And the next day, next week, or next year we want it back! What we missed was that the feeling of liberation came from the cessation of thought that happens moments after the "Ah-ha!" moment because for that brief moment we've stopped thinking and it rids us of our dilemma. For one brief moment, we stop thinking, and it feels WONDERFUL. Freeing. Liberating.

And the moment the feeling passes the Left Hemisphere comes in to craft a story and "take credit" for the blissful feeling. It tries to convince you that the path leading up to the "ah ha" moment was responsible for the bliss. And it's a complete fabrication. The bliss came from the momentary release from thinking that follows the "solution" of a problem. It's a dip into the Right Hemisphere consciousness because the Left Hemisphere hasn't "picked a new target" yet and started its problem solving nonsense which, of course, in order for it to function, must SEE your life as a PROBLEM!! And off you go, and the feeling of bliss from the "ah ha" moment fades with it.And around we go, chasing our tails knowing that if we can only just bite that thing we'll be happy... Just solve this last puzzle and we'll be at rest and in bliss...

It's a complete illusion and a trap that will hold you captive for many many years.

The release came from the cessation of thought, NOT the thought processes that brought you there. So, cut out the middle man and come back to the bliss that is your natural state when still and not "problem solving."

Conceptualizing A Spiritual Method

Zazen sitting meditation (the primary method in Zen) is very simple, once you sit and align your body parts properly, you do nothing, no-thing. And it's one of the hardest and most demanding of all spiritual practices. Humans who are dominated by their Left Hemisphere find doing "no-thing" very challenging. But, what exactly is the challenge!? The challenge is keeping your Left Hemisphere out of the process. The Left Hemisphere is always attempting to "do something." It wants to sniff around and analyze and categorize and it just doesn't have time for this sitting nonsense. It's got important problems to solve...

Even if you do find a way to convince yourself that "being here now" is a good practice (bringing your awareness here, YOU are always here, but I digress...) you will find that the Left Hemisphere will want to "help." But try the following exercise:

Think of the "now." Pretty easy, in fact, pretty boring. It's just that moment that's squeezed between the past and the future. Simple, what's next to think about...

WAIT!!

Now, SENSE the now. What do you hear now? What do you feel now - with your body, not your emotions? What do you smell now? What do you taste now? What do you see now? Don't label anything, just sense.

And then notice the difference between the two exercises, and you will see the difference between a "conceptual exercise" - just thinking of what the "now" is, and an "experiential exercise" - being here now through your senses. They are two totally different things, never let the Left Hemisphere convince you otherwise!

There are many wonderful spiritual exercises invented over the years, and the number one problem people run into with them is that slowly but surely their Left Hemisphere will come in and "conceptualize" the process. I call it "hijacking" or "spiritual hijacking" where it comes in and demands that "this process be taken a different way!" And it's a very subtle thing and many people feel more "comfortable" in a subtle "thinking" state than a state of "no thoughts." And so mistake that familiar feeling with genuine "bliss" and trust me, it's not the same thing. And, after a long time of practicing the "hijacked" version, they give up, certain that "this stuff doesn't work!" This is where a teacher is handy, they can spot this process and make corrections, but even the best teachers can at times be fooled by a student who is just subtly sabotaging the process, so ultimately it's up to you to police the Left Hemisphere and keep it out of your spiritual work.

Chasing External Sources

One of the biggest mistakes we make when approaching spirituality is that we give our power away and it is especially rampant in so called "spiritual seekers." And we are happy to do it, because it takes the responsibility for our peace and bliss off our shoulders, and secretly keeps the Left Hemisphere in control of the ship (by evaluating how effective the external source is in "giving" us the peace "Oh, the stars aren't in line today..." or "The signs are not favorable..." or etc.) It's a subtle and dangerous path, and it's so widespread that it's impossible to list them all. Giving our power away to deities, methods, rituals, magic tricks, science, politics, religions, governments, friends, spiritual teachers, romantic relationships, family members, spouses, drugs, entertainment, sex, oh the list is too long to be comprehensive. And each time we do that we hand the steering wheel of our ship over to something else and sit back and "hope" that it "fixes" us. Of course, included in that list of things we give our power to is problem solving, ruminating, hoping, fearing, judging, etc. etc. etc. But those we've covered. Your power is yours, and it's a LOT greater than you give it credit. In fact ONLY YOU hold any power in your own life. YOU decide, moment to moment what brain functions to feed with your awareness. If you want to feel terrible, you are able to, just feed those brain functions and they will reward you with a terrible feeling. It's that simple. So, when you give your power away, it's like "rolling dice" with your life, if you interpret the external source as positive you will feel good, if you interpret it as negative you won't. And it will be YOU in all cases making that determination. So, cut out the middle man, and take your power back.

Grim Seriousness and Negative Evaluations

There is a prerequisite for the "problem solving" portion of your brain to get access to the rich oxygen blood flow that keeps it going, and that is that your evaluation center gives experiences a "negative" evaluation so the perceived experience, thought, etc. is then a "problem." And of course, what do we do with these problems? Well, we try to find "solutions" so that your problem solving brain functions can feed upon oxygen rich blood and therefore maintain their "high priority status." And there is NO LIMIT to what your brain is able to label as "negative." And therefore, no limit to the number of "problems" you can have in your life. It's up to you. Along with these evaluations comes a grim seriousness, because without it being "very serious" it would not be "high priority" and demand a great amount of blood flow (and the more fed these systems become the greater the demand for blood flow to keep them fed) and so, grim seriousness is the key to keeping the newly labeled "problems" in the forefront of your attention. And it's all crap. Watch out for seriousness, it's a good pointer that you have given your power away to these brain functions. We're all just stardust on this ball of rock in the middle of an enormous universe that is more than likely just one of an infinite number of other universes. What's so serious about our lives? Think of a fly sitting on the end of a hose, and when the water comes out, spending the rest of the day wondering "how did I do that?" That's you in this universe. You're life is not serious. Seriousness is just a process to feed your negative evaluation functions and it kills joy and bliss. It's time to let it go.

The last three of these are little pieces I've previously written, I want to share them with you now. I hope they speak to you:

The Loudest Voice

The problem with dismissing the fact that this so called "path" is really just a re-programming of perception from Primary Left Hemispherical perception to Primary Right Hemispherical Perception is that to not correctly identify the functioning of the Left Hemisphere is to be open to be snared in all kinds of Left Hemisphere traps. If you follow spiritual "methods" and interpret them from the Left Hemisphere as your perception vehicle (because this is your starting point), this tends to prevent you from having an experience of insight (perception through the Right Hemisphere) that will clarify the journey that takes you away from Left Hemisphere's clutches. And since the Left Hemisphere begins this process in control of the ship, it does everything in its power to trick you into keeping it at the helm. And since spiritual methods aren't Left Hemisphere functions, when you misapply them by viewing them through this perception they will ultimately be frustrating and leave one feeling like "this spiritual stuff is a load of crap." If you listen to the propaganda of the Left Hemisphere and evaluate the process through its functions it won't take much time before you're scoffing at folks in "enlightenment groups" discouraging the whole process and laughing at any "suckers" who keep at it.

One of biggest tricks and traps is when the Left Hemisphere attempts (because it's the loudest voice in your head because it controls the language centers of your brain) to "take credit" for each and every experience you perceive. If you have a moment of presence, the Left Hemisphere waits for it to end (presence is that space where you see everything as it is, in this moment) then it "crafts a story" about how you came to "be" present and what processes it takes to "recreate" it in the future, etc. etc. etc. Thus, it tries to take credit for a moment where it was not involved. And we keep buying it. It's like a door to door salesman that we keep buying useless crap from, and we KNOW when it comes to the door that what it has to sell is crap, but we keep buying it because it's the ONLY voice doing the talking. Well, talking aint what it's all about. And those who are still perceiving through the Left Hemisphere as their primary perception vehicle simply can't see the universe any other way than a series of experiences that can be described, cataloged, given a positive or negative value, and placed in a timeline in the "story of me" for future reference. That is the ONLY truth that the Left Hemisphere will BELIEVE because that is how it functions. It is simply unable to give any credence to moments of serene simplicity, where nothing "special" is "happening." However, those moments of simple perception, ARE spiritual practice. None of the talking, or theory, or names, or conceptual identities, or arguments, or jokes, or projections, or categories, or beliefs amount to anything of substance in the practice of "enlightening" your conceptual overlay of that which already is. Not one ounce. Not a sausage. Nada. Zippo.

And yet, in that nothingness, the Left Hemisphere (also known as the "ego") has nothing to do. So, it waits like a stalking predator for the mind to "re-engage" so it can begin the story, the sales pitch, and this time it's a nice "spiritual story" about how you "made it" to "enlightenment." How you meditated until you were one with the "atman" or saw the face of Christ, or Shiva, or Yahweh, or fill in the blank vision one might create through hundreds of hours of focused desire to "achieve" something. And if you focus that much energy into having a vision, well, your mind will eventually create it. It's that simple.

So the key to this begins with identifying the mental processes that will keep you in the Primary Left Hemisphere worldview, that is narrow, argumentative, separate, and certain. And this certainty comes from previous experiences that it "knows" are right because that is the world it understands. That is the world that it has already cataloged and crafted stories about and identified with. That is the world of the concrete truth that it clings to to maintain its conceptual overlay of reality. And it simply can't let go of that certainty, because to do so, to admit that the universe is founded on uncertainty is simply too frightening to the way the Left Hemisphere goes about its business.

Uncertainty leaves it out of the loop. Uncertainty gives it no methods to follow and no icons to worship. Uncertainty means it has to be alert in the moment for ANY possibility. It has to be here, now, and accept everything as it is when it enters its field of perception without pre-fabricated conclusions as to what it's viewing. And that leaves the Left Hemisphere out of the loop. So, while it still has control, it will continue to sell you on its certainty, with a loud blustering confidence, like a politician in a close electoral race, because it knows, that if it shouts the loudest, you will probably keep buying its load of nonsense, and leave it in charge of the ship.

A Special Trap For Spiritual (especially Adviata - or "Non Dualism") Students

Now many people who have read "spiritual books" for many years have fallen into an insidious little trap which I call:

The "I've Solved the Riddle of Awareness" Trap

There is a huge snare in this process that can hold you captive for many years (I know it held me for close to 20 years) and the process is as follows:

1. I feel like an individual in a sea of "others"
2. There are moments when I don't feel so "lonely"
3. Someone introduces me to the concept of "non-duality"
4. I examine it and see, through arguments based in Determinism (*The doctrine that all events, including human action, are ultimately determined by causes external to the will*) that we have no free will in the ultimate sense, because all the particles that make up our bodies and the energy that flows through us are just extensions of the motion created by the Big Bang that were headed on this course on a pre-determined path and will continue long after we're gone on the path it was meant to travel, and all decisions we make

were meant to happen and only we can fill them with a sense that we made them... etc.

5. Satisfied with this the mind (Left Hemisphere) thinks it's got it "all figured out" and uses this as a pat answer to abide in a nihilistic state of "What does it matter!? It's all pre-destined anyway, so no matter what choice I make, it's what I was meant to make, so bring in the dancing girls and put the champagne on ice!"

6. Anytime anyone suggests they examine their own behavior, they bring out the "smoking gun" of "Who is there to examine this behavior!?" or "To consciousness it's all one anyway" etc.

7. As a result of this we continue as egoic self-centered people and generate suffering for ourselves and others behind the shield of "If you suffer, even by my hand, you were meant to suffer!" (This would have been a great argument to fuel the Nazi's by the way!) And go about our merry ways generating karmic explosions wherever we go, smug in our self-righteous certainty that we've "got it all figured out..."

Well, when, as my teacher used to say "You've had enough suffering from this" (missing that if you generate suffering through egocentricity, since we're all one, you generate it for yourself too!!) you get to a place where you are depressed and now you're in a meaningless pre-determined universe in a sea of self created suffering...

And it's hell, let me tell you, it's a hell I don't wish on anyone or anything...

So, what's been missed!? What's been missed in this is the old warning not to use fire to burn fire. Not to use the mind to transcend the mind. This "seeing" has to be taken from the head to the heart. It has to be something brought into your experience, and from this experience, you will laugh at how simple your explanation was. How narrow a vision it was and you will be released from it. But it MUST be seen from a different point of view (through the perception of the Right Hemisphere) to be seen in its entirety and then ultimately, when the laughter ceases from how funny it is to watch the Left Hemisphere in its certainty, you will open to an entirely NEW universe, where determinism is only a small part of the play (like the difference between

Newtonian Universe – determinism – and the Einsteinian Universe - Relativity.) It's an eye opening thing to see, and from this relative view you can either see the universe as deterministic, OR a completely free place to create in the present moment through intentions that lead us on a ride that's a wonderful (full of wonder) place to be! Joy fills your heart and you don't just LABEL others as "part of the one" you KNOW from direct experience that they are, and you lose all desires to harm, berate, or feel superior to them because it is just a silly notion to harm oneself. Not because of any "concept" you have about the "oneness" of things, but by the same process that you wouldn't harm your own body... You love your neighbor as yourself in mind, body, spirit, and deed, not just with your thoughts.

Lastly, I want to share with you a little bit I wrote about the voice in our heads that when I wrote it made me laugh:

The Loud Drunk

The Left Hemisphere of your brain is like a loud drunk in a crowded room. Always ready to tell you who you are and what you should be doing. But like the loud drunk, it's rarely worth taking seriously...

How to De-Stimulate Limbic Conditioning (and Pain Body Strategies)

"I may not be in total control of what happens to my life but I certainly am in charge of how I choose to perceive my experience."

- Jill Bolte Taylor Ph.D.

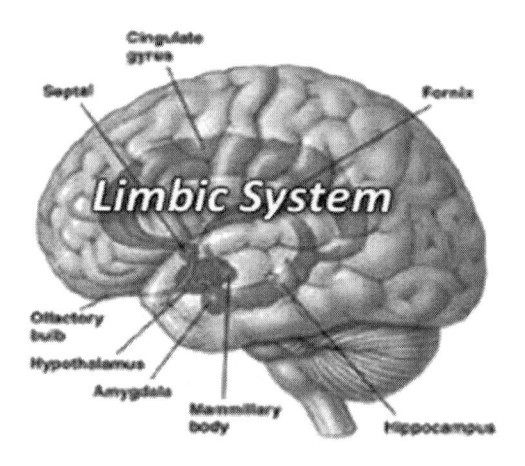

When the "Pain Body" strikes it comes with great force. It carries with it the full force of the emotions we've been denying, and like the voice of a jilted lover, it won't be ignored any longer. Because they were us. They are echoes in the present of what we should have felt in moments past, but weren't present enough to feel. So the only way out of this is to give them their due, feel them fully, and then set them free. However, the payment will never be more than 90 seconds (thanks to Dr. Taylor for mentioning this!), because anything after that is excess compensation. The Pain Body is the most powerful conditioned response but it's the least stable state because it needs both aspects of its duel-natured existence to be ignored in order for it to continue. The Pain Body is comprised of a thought or memory and an emotional residue from that memory, and if either of them is allowed, or surrendered to completely, then the Pain Body must disperse. That means, that if a Pain Body attack comes, you can either surrender to the memory fully (allow it, for how can a memory EVER change, it's like watching the same movie over and over and hoping for a different ending) or you can just feel the emotion fully, and let it run its course, without engaging in the triggered thought again to re-spark it.

Now the Pain Body is a stubborn little high priority system, and it won't go without a fight. Just like its cohort, the Left Hemisphere, it will continue to "pop up" asking each time "are you sure you're done with this!?" In time, when you allow the memories fully, the pain body will switch strategies to your dreams and try to "play themselves out" there. Once you allow that your dreams will "be what they are" but that you will no longer "follow them" by obsessing over the content the next day, it will then switch to just sending "emotions" without any memory, hoping that the emotion itself will prompt you to wonder "why you're feeling it" and you will do the work for it and attach a thought or memory to it. Don't feel like you're insane when this happens, when for some reason you suddenly feel a wave of "melancholy" come over you for no reason, just notice it, and know that this is a great sign. This means that The Pain Body is desperate and trying ANYTHING to spark you into a full episode. Just allow it, and laugh at its attempts, even speak to it reassuringly if you need to, say "Thank you, I know you're trying to do what you think is best for me, but I don't need this gift right now..." and let it go.

In time these little episodes will subside, and by feeling what you feel always fully, and not "chasing mental movies" you will slowly dissipate this process. Remember, don't chase the memories or thoughts, feel what you feel now, then let it go, and you will ultimately just settle into what you are always, which is what you are right now. I wrote a little piece about this I hope it speaks to you:

90 Seconds To Peace

If an emotional state enters your body, it only take 90 seconds to flush out the chemicals involved. This is, of course, if the emotion is not re-triggered through playing out the triggering mechanism in our minds over and over by mental obsessing. So, remember, no matter what emotion you're feeling you are only 90 seconds away from peace! If you are struggling with letting it be by relaxing through accepting your present moment, even counting slowly to 90 will be better than replaying emotional stories in your mind! Let the story go and the body takes care of itself naturally.

On hallucinogens and the Pineal Gland

The pineal gland is a small endocrine gland in the Limbic System of our brains. It produces the serotonin derivative melatonin, a hormone that affects the modulation of wake/sleep patterns and seasonal functions. René Descartes dedicated much time to the study of the pineal gland, and called it the "principal seat of the soul." He believed it to be the point of connection between the intellect and the body. Today the exact function of the Pineal Gland and its link to mystical states of consciousness are in great debate and there is much speculation to its connection to the tryptophan family of hallucinogens.

HOW TO DE-STIMULATE LIMBIC CONDITIONING (AND PAIN BODY STRATEGIES)

The use of hallucinogens in spiritual practice is as old as spiritual practices themselves. No one doubts their profoundly influential and impactful experiences on the users. However, in terms of liberation, it is my personal opinion that they offer little or no benefit in terms of touching what is always available to us in our peaceful brain wiring. However, the ONE exception to this is that the perceptions that they generate are so outside of what we have identified as "ours" that they are a direct experience of our own conditioning as it comes back to the forefront of our consciousness as the effects of the hallucinogen wears off. And as such can be an excellent pointer to the fact that we experience just ONE of virtually infinite possible perceptions that this universe (possibly multiverse) has to offer. In that one aspect alone, I am not against their usage. As a crutch, or in place of actual work, I see them as a potential detriment to the process which can be done from a baseline mental state with no enhancements needed whatsoever.

How to Stimulate Right Hemisphere Functions

"The main theme to emerge... is that there appear to be two modes of thinking, verbal and nonverbal, represented rather separately in Left and Right Hemispheres respectively and that our education system, as well as science in general, tends to neglect the nonverbal form of intellect. What it comes down to is that modern society discriminates against the Right Hemisphere."

- Roger Sperry

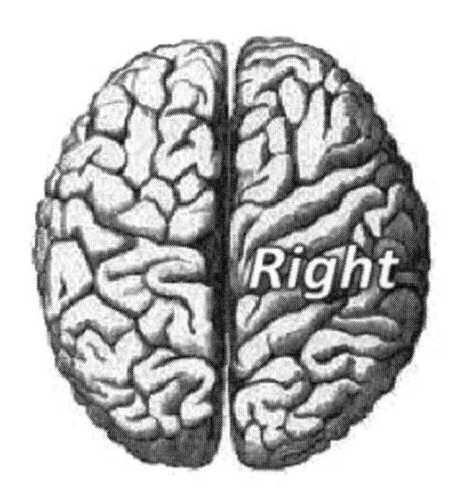

So modern man has built a temple to the Left Hemisphere in this world we're living in, but that doesn't mean it's a cage with no exits. We hold the key, and can release ourselves at any moment. I hear you say "but I don't know how!" it is ironic that that certainty alone is what is holding you back. For you are always here, only your thoughts can convince you otherwise. That being said, there are many many wonderful methods that have been created over the years, I could never list them all in this book, and would recommend seeking out a teacher if you would like to master any of the more refined meditation techniques available. I am going to discuss in general how one can "switch hemispherical perception" and activate Right Hemisphere functions. It's up to you to do the work, no one can do this work for you, and this work IS SPIRITUALITY!! Not reading more books, or listening to more Satsangs by your favorite teacher (though just listening to a teacher who speaks from presence is quite useful), it's about being here now, fully. I'm going to start with something I wrote myself before moving onto discuss other techniques:

How To Enter the Right Hemisphere

The method by which we "step to the right of the Left Hemisphere" is to engage the external and internal stimulus that the Right Hemisphere is designed to perceive. As it turns out, most meditative practices are meant to do just this.

1. Soften your vision (or close your eyes if you are too distracted by visual "labeling" at first)
2. Feel and listen to your internal body
3. Stay very alert, but don't attach the alertness to any concept or object

4. Don't follow mental stories or labels, just allow them, in fact the act of just "observing them" without labeling them (often called Observation Meditation) is simply the Right Hemisphere examining the Left Hemisphere and is the act by which the bulk of meditation is practiced.
5. If you want to play sound or music when you do this, the music should be without lyrics to decrease the impact on the language center. If you throw in nature sounds (birds chirping, water flowing, waves crashing, etc.) the Right Hemisphere will be engaged UNLESS you begin to single out and label any of the sounds.
6. Boredom as a sensation means you're making progress, and the Left Hemisphere is not getting enough stimuli, this is where most people trip up and can go no further, because DEEP boredom feels like a kind of "death." And in fact, it is a form of death, it's the Left Hemisphere losing blood flow by being de-prioritized, and since we hold our sense of "self" in there when we begin this process, it will feel as if the "YOU" as you perceive yourself to be at this moment, will start to fade. In order to stop this function the Left Hemisphere will shoot "fear" into the system (fear is a state where we see ourselves as separate and it's a way to keep us in our Left-Hemisphere identified state) which is meant to "shock you" back into its clutches. In time you will see it coming and by allowing it fully, get past it.
7. This "sending fear" technique will be a constant attempt by the Left Hemisphere as you continue to master this process, allow it fully and in time it will actually be funny to watch as it tries to "trick you" into identifying with it, but ask it a question "If you are so real, why do you need tricks for me to see you?" It doesn't like that question and has no answer…

This is a good start for those interested. I can't say how this compares with meditation techniques that others use, this is what I use throughout the day (sometimes I sit and 'formally meditate'), but this can be done anywhere and anytime.

Here is another piece I wrote on this subject:

The Method

One of the primary functions of the Left Hemisphere of the brain is problem solving. Very little of one's day is spent solving actual problems. The remainder of the time the Left Hemisphere spends manufacturing false problems, so it can continue the function.

The way out of this habit is through the application of simple awareness. Allow your awareness to become hyper-engaged yet unattached, then move that awareness into your body. This is the technique I use for simple awareness. I highly recommend it as a short break many times during your day. I hope it serves you.

Through The Senses

The most direct pathway to the Right Hemisphere is through the senses. If you focus on what you feel, taste, hear, smell, and see right here, right now, without labeling any of it just focus on the experience of it, and you are headed into the Right Hemisphere. Sense but don't label as you:

- Walk in nature, listen to the sounds, view the sights.
- Smell your food, breathe it in deeply, then taste it fully as you eat it. Do the same with what you drink.
- Feel how your clothes touch your body. Feel the wind in your hair. Are you cold? Hot?
- Listen to a beautiful piece of music, without lyrics, just listen, don't follow any thoughts it provokes.

Simply sense what you experience now. And you will be drawing upon the perception of the Right Hemisphere. At first these connections will be weak, but as you continue to use them they will strengthen and take you places you never even know existed.

4 Basic Meditation Techniques

I'd like to go over four basic meditation techniques. If you are interested in any of them there are many sources for a more detailed description and many teachers that can walk you through them in a systematic and useful way. These descriptions are meant to be illustrative not comprehensive, and to give you a glimpse of the many pathways to our Right Hemisphere consciousness.

<u>Observation Meditation</u>

Sit and watch your thoughts. It is VERY important to not JUDGE the thought, just watch it. Like a cloud passing by without saying "That's a nice cloud" or "That's a terrible cloud" etc. Just watch the thoughts and it will slowly teach you how to increase the space between you and them, also when watching the thoughts that pass in the present moment you are IN the present moment and in touch with the processes of the Right Hemisphere. Remember Do not judge your thoughts, or evaluate them in any way, if you do it is not Observation Meditation, it is just another form of rumination. Allow them to be fully, and let them go.

This is an excellent method for beginners to see clearly the fundamental principle that "they are not their thoughts" and is the primary method in all meditation techniques to "create space" between you and your thoughts.

<u>Inner Body/Breath Meditation</u>

Close your eyes. Feel your internal body, and follow it as far and as deeply as you can. Lift your hands from touching any surface, and ask yourself a simple question as you begin:

"How do I know I have hands?"

And allow your awareness to move to your hands. As you do, at first you will not be able to feel much, maybe a tingling, or a pulsing sensation, move your awareness throughout your body. At the end attempt to hold the entire body in a feeling of sensation in the present moment. Add breath work to the process to deepen the sensation (even out your breath, if you have to count at first to 4 for your in breath, then 4 for your out breath, then move it to 6 and then to 8.) This brings you into the present moment and forces your brain to prioritize Right Hemisphere functions, etc.

This is Eckhart Tolle's favored method.

"I am" meditation

Focus on the SENSATION "I Am" not the thought. Do not allow your mind to answer the question in ANY WAY or give you ANY CONCEPT OR SENSATION to answer the question (the question of what "I am.") Follow it as far as you are able and be brave in doing so. Let nothing derail you from the journey or convince you of what "I Am" is outside of the sensation alone.

This was a favorite of Ramana Maharshi and Nisargadatta Maharaj, two great Indian Sages.

Zazen

Zazen is a posture and a method of breathing, and is a primary method in the Zen tradition. It is very useful because the posture is so hard to hold properly that it takes a beginner's full concentration, thus forcing them to do nothing but it if they wish to do it well. In time, when they master the posture, they will be able to sit and do nothing, "no-thing." You can attempt this without the posture by sitting and doing "no-thing" but you will find it very frustrating and hard to do. Ironic isn't it, that in the end doing nothing is much harder than doing anything else!

There are many fine Zen monasteries and teachers that would be more than willing to walk you through Zazen, if that method speaks to you.

There are literally thousands more meditation techniques in the world, this is but a few of the most common. In the end, I have found that they all have as their goal (though most don't know it) the merging of our awareness with our peaceful Right Hemisphere consciousness.

The Process

A noted calligrapher asked Tesshu what method he followed.

"No method."

"I don't understand."

"Which do you think is the better carpenter: one who can only work with exactly the right tools, or the one who can make do with whatever is on hand?"

Blood Flow

For over 20 years I've read material on Eastern Spirituality. I've also, for many years been an avid reader of psychological and scientific material, with a special interest in brain mechanics. Last year, a profound change came over the way in which I perceived reality on a day to day basis, and, coupled with the many years study the change came primarily from following the advice of Eckhart Tolle and understanding brain mechanics at a much deeper level due to the works of Dr. Jill Bolte Taylor. I've done nothing in this last year but practice, study, and teach and in that year the one thing that has come to be clearly the center piece of this entire subject matter is blood flow. The cells of the human brain are all alive, and they gain energy to reproduce through oxygen rich blood. The more we call to focus their functions from where we place our awareness, the more the oxygen rich blood flows to those cells and the neural net grows. The more it grows, the more blood it needs to maintain its size, and so it demands more and more of your perception to sustain. I've learned that there are many strategies that the various portions of your brain will undertake to convince you of their need, the goal of which is to subtlety nudge you into sending that oxygen rich blood their way so they can feed. There are drawbacks to this, primarily that some of these brain functions make daily life less than pleasant as an experience. This was evidenced in Dr. Jill Bolte Taylor's reply when asked why she shunned the return of anger into her daily perception quite profoundly when she said flatly:

"I didn't like the way it felt in my body..."

We all share that feeling, and when we foster these less than pleasant perceptions we gain with them the less than pleasant physical and mental states that accompany them. The Buddha called this process "Dukkha" or suffering. And he noticed over 2600 years ago that when we no longer fed those portions of our brain, and instead nurtured the portions that generated love, joy, bliss, compassion, and a sense of being one with our environment, that profound changes occurred in how we experienced incoming stimulus. He called it "Liberation" it's also been termed "Enlightenment." So, what is the process by which this is done? I'll restate again in brief:

You are always here. The process is to merge your awareness with you. That's it.

Ok, how do we "do" that? Well there are many methods and we'll discuss some here. Don't mistake the methods for the peace. They are only pointers to what you really are, they aren't what you are.

The Wave and the Ocean Metaphor Unveiled

The metaphor of the wave and the ocean is as old as spiritual teachings themselves, and there is a reason for this, it's an excellent example of the nature of the merging of the form based reality (the wave) and the ultimate reality (the ocean) of which it (the wave) is separate from and simultaneously never leaves. I used this metaphor myself earlier in the book, and have used it many times as an excellent illustration of the reality that we are both form and non-form simultaneously. Now, we need only take it one step further and that is to understand that in order for us to hold both diversely different worldviews in one space (our brains) we needed two different brains that see the world in those two important yet separate ways. And, we have just the thing. The Left Hemisphere sees the world as separate little forms (wave consciousness) while the Right Hemisphere sees everything as part of one large "one-ness" (ocean consciousness.) As it turns out, when we access the ocean consciousness we are at peace and feel a great sense of bliss and love. When we are in wave consciousness we feel isolated, vulnerable (ready to crash onto the shore at any moment), and stressful. So, the key is to use the wave consciousness only when the environment forces us to, otherwise to abide in the peaceful and bliss-filled ocean consciousness, and use it to guide our lives effortlessly through reality.

And now onto the "method" that I still use on a daily basis. Let me forewarn you it cannot be practiced in "half measures" (the first step is by far the hardest) and it's not the only "method" known to man, but from my experience it's the most effective way to bring peace to this present moment.

Forgive, Accept, Release, Relax

"Whatever you accept completely will take you to peace, including the acceptance that you cannot accept, that you are in resistance."

- Eckhart Tolle

When we are on this path we will find that we stumble upon conditioned (high-priority status) patterns of thinking and behavior that were once "unconscious" (guiding our behavior without our knowledge) and are now "conscious" and able to be let go. The path to freedom, no matter what the starting point (i.e. whether it's a thought in the form of a belief or certainty, a behavior, an emotion, etc.), no matter what the obstacle, begins with these four steps:

Forgive:
Everything is a product of its karma. How could it be any different?
There's nothing/no one to blame.

Accept:
Accept what is. Exactly as it is. It is what it is, why resist what already is?

Release:
It's not you. Let it go, spread your arms to the wind and release it from your life.

Relax:
Access the joy and peace circuitry in your brain.

None of these concepts are new. None of this is outside of your personal experience. In fact, nothing any of the great sages have been saying for thousands of years is complicated. In fact it is deceptively simple. So simple, that it's hard. If you find, after doing these four steps, that the obstacle remains retrace the steps and see which one was not followed completely. The Left Hemisphere will "yeah yeah..." things or "fake" or just "rush through" things and convince itself that it "did the work." Don't fall for that nonsense. Embrace each step as if your life depended on it. It does. The caliber of your life depends on how deeply and fully you are able to release yourself from the bondage that holds you. And the holder of the strings is ALWAYS YOU. There is no external source needed for the sensation of the greatest bliss and peace.

Counter "Intuitive"

I think one of the most important things to notice in the process is something so fundamental that it's rarely spoken about. My teacher taught it to me through one simple phrase he would ask me "So, how is that working for you Mark?" And it would frustrate me and send me away in a huff. What he was pointing to is that much of the processes that we currently think are the answers to our "problems" if they have failed to create peace and bliss in our lives, MUST be creating problems not solving them. As I began to apply the material in my practice, much of what I experienced about liberation on the surface felt "counter intuitive." However, that feeling was really inaccurate, it wasn't counter "intuitive" what it really was was "counter to my programming" and the new practices accessed brain functions that I had not previously "invested with a sense of self" and so they felt "odd" or "off" at first.

When the Left Hemisphere dominates our perception, we don't even know what genuine intuition is, and we mistake "not feeling like us" for "counter intuitive." In the end, when examined, it's pretty simple, the processes that build conditioning are destroyed by their opposites. This is why practice is SO IMPORTANT. It's about "experiencing it yourself" but REALLY trying it, not just dipping your toe in and saying you "tried swimming" get in and splash about. After awhile, through application, you "get the feel for it" and then in time you will be the one with a lack of words to describe what can only be experienced firsthand.

So if Forgive, Accept, Release, Relax destroys conditioning, what built it? Well what built it was:

Judge
Critique, scrutinize, weigh, examine.

Evaluate
Assign value to - e.g. generate attachment to (positive evaluation) or resist (negative evaluation)

Hold
Invest the evaluation with a sense of self (e.g. "my thought"/"my belief"/"my experience")

Stress
Ruminate, fantasize, obsess over, make stories about

So I'm going to ask you now:

"How have these four processes worked for you so far?"

It's time to do the opposite, and no longer assemble but destroy what these processes have built.

I'm going to go over the new steps now one by one to better explain what is expected, but before I do, I want to say that when I showed these four steps to my teacher he said:

"Great steps, but you're going to have a hard time getting people to do the first one…"

And so, I want to make a specific challenge to you, I challenge you to find the space to:

Forgive

"When you forgive, you in no way change the past - but you sure do change the future."

- Bernard Meltzer

What could have happened differently? Given that the path that all the energy took from the Big Bang to the present moment came as it did, what exactly could have happened differently? What alternate scenario was SUPPOSED to happen exactly? How was that person supposed to behave differently than what their environments and conditioning influenced them to behave? Have they done the work and seen that they are not their thoughts!? Have they released themselves through daily practice and application from their painful conditioning? Are they or ANYONE perfect in their behavior in terms of what is "good" or "bad" behavior? And so what are you holding onto? What SHOULD they have done differently? What SHOULD have your life been? Was there a chance that your personal conditioning and environment would have made a different you? Was there a chance that you had different parents, siblings, or social status? What SHOULD have been different to make you who you are right now? How can obsessing over the details of the past effect the present in any way other than causing grief and suffering? What SHOULD have you been? They been? You acted? They acted? Done judging yet? Had enough time to evaluate and categorize? Or is the Left Hemisphere saying "just a little more..." "just one more thought about this and we'll drop it..." "just one more..." "just one more..."

Let it go.

No one, and nothing, could be anything but what it is. Let go, and forgive. You are only causing yourself and others suffering by holding onto "shoulds" and "shouldn'ts." It's over. Let go. Feel any feelings that have been unfelt, FULLY. Find a safe place and let go.

The only one holding onto this painful baggage is you now. It's done. It's gone. Let it go. Why would anyone want to hold on to something like this!? Aren't there better things to hold in this wonderful universe!?

It's time to let go, the past has no claim on you, or effect on the present moment. Even physical limitations caused by past moments have nothing to do with this present moment. This moment you are what you are, you have what you have, and nothing changes that. Be here now. That's where you always are, so bring your awareness to YOU and out of your head.

It's time. Forgive it fully. Hold nothing back. Release it to the universe, it's in safe hands. There is only the now. And, most importantly, if you find you are unable to forgive, make sure to forgive yourself first, for not being able to forgive.

Accept

*"We cannot change anything until we accept it.
Condemnation does not liberate, it oppresses."*

- Carl Jung

No matter what we're thinking about, fantasizing about, dreaming about, hoping was different, the one thing that that act can NEVER do is change the present moment.

We can fantasize that we are in a far off land, dream that we are in paradise and that our situations and problems are elsewhere, we can fantasize about being another person in another life, our imaginations can do almost anything EXCEPT change the present moment.

It already is.

I ask my many religious friends, one simple question:

"What mistake did God make in bringing you this moment?"

Accept what is.

I want to share with you now a script I wrote for a video I made, I hope it speaks to you:

<u>The Already Viewed Film</u>

If we sit down to watch a movie we've already viewed it's quite a different sensation from the first time we've seen it. We sit and the story moves past our senses but in the back of our mind we know where it is going, so we're less "caught up" in the plot to a slight degree because we can always "step back" and say "Oh yeah, she's going to be fine in the end, I don't need to be so frightened..." or in the case of say the movie "Titanic", we can let go of the resistance to the boat sinking, because, we KNOW from viewing the film, that it WILL sink, whether we wish it to or not. Something inside us allows us to have an internal dialogue in the nature of:

> "Oh, I don't want them to die, but they are going to die, I know because I've seen this before, so I can just let go of that resistance and just watch the movie..."

We disengage the story teller that wants to "re-write" the script because we KNOW that no amount of desire will change the outcome of the movie. We know how it will end, and there's no need to create an additional amount of pain by resisting the ending of the already painful story portrayed in the film.

We can, if we choose, just be a witness to what's going on, and allow the story to continue to an ending we know is inevitable. Stress drops greatly and we can just munch on popcorn, even in the scary parts…

Well as it turns out, our lives are exactly the same way. The only sensation that is in real time, in this present moment, is the sensation that you are. EVERY other sensation that streams through the senses comes from the past. It's the not too distant past, no doubt, but the past nonetheless. If you perceive it, it's already happened. The fastest speed in this universe is the speed of light, and yet it still takes time to move through the universe. Anything you sense through your sensory systems moves through electrical impulses at the speed of light from the point of contact to your brain and then registers as an impulse in the moment. The moment where you sense "I am." By the time you sense the impulse it's already fixed and final and unchangeable. It already IS.

So, like the film, you are viewing something that has already happened, and just like the film you've already seen, you have the option of letting go of resistance and "just watching the movie" (abiding in the self, resting as awareness, etc. etc. etc.) and allowing your natural intelligence to respond in the moment how it feels best suits the information it's been given. It's the most efficient method to deal with this paradox of living in the now and sensing only the past. If you're always already behind the curve, why resist such a truth, it would be better to just turn and go with the wave. Ironically, when you do that, you gain the momentum of the entire universe as your ally, and it takes you, always, where you need to be.

"What could be more futile, more insane than to generate inner resistance to something that already is?" – Eckhart Tolle

Release

*"We must let go of the life we have planned,
so as to accept the one that is waiting for us."*

- Joseph Campbell

Are you ever going to be anyone/thing but you? After you die you will be you dead, and no one knows what that means or what that experience will hold. No matter what they say or what experiences with the afterlife they've had. It's still just belief and conjecture.

You are you, here and now. It's time to let go of everything else. No one can let go of this but you. You have to let go of the certainty that holds this to you and release it fully. It's not you. It's a mental construct in your head, let it go. Let the idea of you, or of them/it go. You/they/or it are NOT the idea. It's time to stop carrying this burden. It's excess and unneeded cargo. Let it go.

Spread your arms to the universe and release this surplus weight. En-LIGHTEN yourself now! The only thing that can convince you that you are loaded down in this manner is thinking, you are not your thoughts, let go.

It's time. And the time is always:
now.

Relax

"All differences in this world are of degree, and not of kind, because oneness is the secret of everything."

- Swami Vivekananda

Relax into the freedom that is your birthright. Let go of all concepts and thoughts. Feel your inner body. Smell the air. Hear the sounds. Look out without labeling what you see. This is you. As you are. Only thoughts can convince you differently, let them go. Tap into the consciousness of your Right Hemisphere and sense this wondrous universe that is, in the end, just you.

Let go and relax into you.

Deconditioning Takes Time, and it can only happen in the Now

"Unconscious people – and many remain unconscious, trapped in their egos throughout their lives – will quickly tell you who they are: their name, their occupation, their personal history, the shape or state of their body, and whatever else they identify with. Others may appear to be more evolved because they think of themselves as an immortal soul or living spirit. But do they really know themselves, or have they just added some spiritual sounding concepts to the content of their mind? Knowing yourself goes far deeper than the adoption of a set of ideas or beliefs. Spiritual ideas and beliefs may at best be helpful pointers, but in themselves they rarely have the power to dislodge the more firmly established core concepts of who you think you are, which are part of the conditioning of the human mind. Knowing yourself deeply has nothing to do with whatever ideas are floating around in your mind. Knowing yourself is to be rooted in Being, instead of lost in your mind."

- Eckhart Tolle

The Journey

When you begin this journey you know that you are special and unique. When you see past specialness you see that everyone is unique and know they should all be treated fairly. When you see past fairness you let go of fair in place of what is true. When you see past truth you let go of truth in place of what is real. When you see past reality you let go of reality in place of what can be sensed. When you see past the senses you let go of perception in place of the limit of what it is to be human. When you see past the limitations of being human you join the rest of the universe as one non special non independent whole. And as this whole you are again special and unique.

Unraveling a conditioned behavior

When practicing ridding oneself of a behavior that one has noticed through awareness, it's important to be patient and non-judgmental (if you judge yourself you just add suffering on top of a process that needs none to work perfectly.)

My experience of this is that the entire process is handled with simple awareness. Accepting what is, then watching it with non-judgmental viewing. It's important to remember that this takes time, it doesn't go away immediately. There is a process and a progression which I would like to share from my experience and it goes as follows:

1. You are completely unaware of the process
2. You notice the process in hindsight (well after the event has passed)
3. You notice the process JUST after finishing (shaking your head wondering why...)

4. You notice the process mid way through it and have the option of stopping it in the middle of the process and dropping it
5. You notice the process JUST before it begins and a Y appears in the road offering you a choice of going down the same old road, or choosing another path.
6. You notice the triggers for the process as they show up and the feelings begin to stir, and you let go of them immediately
7. You notice the build up to the triggers and are completely prepared for the situation and let go before ANYTHING arises
8. The process disappears from your life completely.

It is important to notice that the first time that the word "choice" appears is in step 5. Steps 1-4 are what Eckhart Tolle likes to term "various degrees of unconsciousness." And by "unconscious" he does not mean asleep, he means that we are not fully conscious of the conditioned process and have no meaningful control over it. In fact, most people because they live Socrates' "unexamined life" never get past step 1. If you are in step 5 and you choose to go down the old pathway don't judge yourself for it. Sometimes it's important to go down that pathway "consciously" and watch how it feels. This gives us a clearer vision of it and helps us toward the later steps. Judgment never does anything but add a layer of pain to what might already be a painful process. It NEVER works. Forgive yourself completely, and join with Christ in finally understanding fully what he meant when on the cross he said:

"Father, forgive them, for they know not what they do."

Christ, a very conscious being, knew that those who were harming him were merely products of their conditioning and forgave them fully. How can you hold people accountable for behavior they don't even understand or see? The behavior owns them, they don't own it. Forgive yourself for being where you are, judgment slows down the process and adds unneeded suffering.

This is the progression so never fear, it takes time and patience to re-wire. The tool with which we accomplish this is through simple non-judgmental (Right Hemisphere based) awareness and then your natural intelligence will do the rest (through observation the brain will re-value it all on its own.)

If the behavior includes a partner, then once you are out of the loop, your partner will have no one to dance with, and will have the option of re-examining the behavior themselves and one of two things will happen:

1. They will be unsatisfied and look for another partner to continue the dynamic
2. They will be released from it as well and follow you to freedom.

Enlightened Relationships

"A genuine relationship is one that is not dominated by the ego with its image-making and self-seeking. In a genuine relationship, there is an outward flow of open, alert attention toward the other person in which there is no wanting whatsoever."

- Eckhart Tolle

Everyone is where they are supposed to be as a product of the energy they are comprised of and its journey through this amazing universe. The key to loving another is accepting them completely as they are with your whole heart. This does not mean that if they are harmful to you you need to accept the abuse, it means accept them, as they are, right now, without any idea that they should be anything but what they are now. Because they can be nothing else. Or to put it more succinctly:

"By accepting you as you are, I do not necessarily abandon all hope of your improving."
- Ashleigh

All effective action comes from accepting what is, and this is even more important when it is another person, because all resistance to who they are just creates an added barrier between you and them and makes all meaningful progress between you two impossible. You are not responsible for who they are or how they behave no matter what your relationship to them is. If you love someone deeply the first step you must take to show them genuine love is to release them from your judgments, and from your negative behaviors. In the end, that is the only gift we are capable of giving another. Work on YOU and let them be. If you free them from you, you give them the first opportunity they've ever had to examine freedom themselves.
"It takes two to tango..."
Stop dancing, and see what happens...

Difficult and Deeply Unconscious People

Difficult and deeply unconscious people serve a great function in God's universe. They have chosen to be far from God, a genuine sacrifice, so that we might learn from their unconsciousness. Without them as opposites, we would never perceive true inner spiritual existence. Their sacrifice is deeply sacred and we should honor them with love and acceptance at all times. For without them, there would be no enlightenment.

What No One Tells You

The shift of hemispheres from Left to Right is what was referred to in years past (because they didn't actually know the process that they were enacting on a neuroanatomical level) as: Enlightenment, Nirvana, Christ Nature, Buddha Nature, The Tao, and many others. It's a wonderful and life altering process, however the Karma of the act of Enlightenment is that those who have very strong "Victim Identities" or those who have very strong "Superiority Complexes" might want to get away from you. This is because your existence outside of the realm of "good and bad" and "right and wrong" is a threat to their self created personas. This means that slowly but surely they might leave your life because you are simply too threatening to remain around... And this could be a spouse, life-long close friend, or family member.

However, also, suddenly many people that you never even noticed before will be "strangely drawn" to you and seek out your company and your thoughts. There is Karma in all actions. Often, in the "Enlightenment Game" they don't speak of this, it's not a good "sales pitch" and won't sell a lot of books... I am here to tell you however, it's well worth it!!

No, with love

Some of the greatest challenges we face with family and old friends are their expectations of being able to violate healthy boundaries. It is important as you progress down this path, that you enforce rock solid boundaries, with love. I call the energy "no, with love." And the key is to hold the boundary like a diamond wall, and the energy that holds it is the love you give (remember the definition of love is to accept something as it is completely with your whole heart.) No energy is more powerful than love and so all other energies in time have to rise to meet it or run away to maintain their lower frequencies. Gandhi proved this to the entire British Empire, he simply said to them "No, with love" and in time they accepted that his boundaries were healthy and rock solid. If this can be done at that level, then at the level of just one little family, it should be child's play, right!? If only it were that simple. Well, the process is the same anyway, the outcome will depend on how threatening the gesture is to those who will have to deal with it. Forgive them fully, that is the beginning of the power of the love that will hold your boundaries solid. And remember, as you do, to keep in mind the quote from Ram Dass:

> *"If you think you're enlightened, go spend a week with your family..."*

Be The Change

I hear you, I do:

> *"But I love them and I want to help them!"*

No one can hear what they are not ready to hear. This information cannot be forced on another person. If you are unable to allow them to be as they are they will never feel comfortable enough to ask questions about your changes. In fact, as you become a more peaceful, patient, and loving person, that alone will be a profoundly impactful lesson to them. Much more impactful in fact than handing them this or any book, or lecturing them on how "unconscious" they are. You have to have patience and love even their unconscious behavior, that is who they are right now, and they deserve your love. Don't feed it, but don't give it negative energy either. Accept it, and give them love. If their behavior crosses healthy boundaries, enforce your boundaries firmly and lovingly. I call this "No, with love." Firmly is VERY important, and lovingly is the only possible way of influencing them positively. In the end, we are all responsible for our own behavior and not for anyone else's. If we want change in this world we must follow Gandhi's advice:

"You must be the change you want to see in the world."

Some Essays

*"Flow with whatever may happen and let your mind be free.
Stay centered by accepting whatever you are doing.
This is the ultimate."*

- Chuang Tzu

I want to share some essays I've written about accessing the perception through the Right Hemisphere and the Spiritual Process in general, I hope they speak to you:

The Present Is Freedom

As a tool the Left Hemisphere of the brain needs the past and future to function. It is a linear calculating machine and needs the concepts of previous and post to align the present thought into a value based category. The present moment offers it nothing to grasp onto. Therefore, the freedom from its clutches comes from embracing the present moment. Feel it, touch it, smell it, hear it, see it and you're free.

How to Ride the Now

There are many things that the universe is completely at ease within that human language and concepts cannot penetrate and one of those things is a paradox. The universe functions perfectly well within paradoxes like:

> *"It takes time to become enlightened, and it can only happen in the now."*

and

> *"We exist in a world of form, real, vibrant, alive and pulsing, and it is an illusion of the senses."*

also,

"There is nothing to do to reach reality, and yet without great effort in the pursuit of this not doing, we will not come to embrace it fully."

What happens here is that the method of "noticing that everything is already perfect" is an excellent pointer to that perception where judgment is excluded (the Right Hemispherical view.) Categories are gone and separateness is an illusion. Simple non judgmental viewing, and the acceptance of everything as it is. When describing this perception of reality it is often mistaken for a singular moment that is then "finished in its perfection" and then by noticing it something is then "accomplished." This misses the reality that there are no singular moments, there are pulses of choice within this flow, and within each pulse this view must be maintained by force of will at first (willful nonjudgmental viewing, as judgmental/category based viewing "the Left Hemispherical view - will be the default at first, however by noticing that judgmental perception moment to moment you will open a gateway out of that habit/conditioning" the reason for this is that by using the nonjudgmental viewing to notice the judgmental viewing you are in fact engaging the Right Hemisphere to notice the Left! And this IS practice in the use of the Right Hemisphere!) and then less and less willpower will be required through "getting the feel for it" as the waves of pulse progress (kind of like learning how to surf, not falling in the moment is essential, and yet it takes time to learn how to do so, and the universe is filled with many waves of energy, how well we learn to "ride" them will ultimately determine how "smooth" the journey is...) And there lies the paradox that our linear minds have trouble embracing and that is that there are no singular moments and yet time progresses. And, while this makes no linear logical sense to our minds, the universe has no problem functioning perfectly within it. Each singular pulse/wave that we "sense" is really all one large "now moment" as all waves are really just part of the sea. Within that large moment there are pulses where we may choose this or that. Follow this path or that path in an infinite pool of choices of "timelines/waves without end or breaks" (kind of like jumping from wave to wave, but no wave can "hold you" and yet none of them stop or even pause.) Time is not linear, it is instead one large "pool" of possibilities and inside of that non linear pool, we, from pulse wave to pulse wave, choose to face one direction or another and that points us in a new unending path of potentiality.

What does this mean in practical terms?

It means you need to practice to keep this view vibrant, and the practice is a simple non judgmental viewing of that which is (Where are my feet on this surfboard? How is my balance right now?), which can be called "perfect" in any singular moment as a pointer to let go of judgmental viewing which just adds a layer of concepts over what is, and clouds clear vision and creates a "rough ride."

The Left Hemisphere Tool in This Search

The one area where the Left Hemisphere is helpful in a spiritual journey is in the elimination of singular concepts through simple logic. For instance, that there is no past and no future. Through simple deduction one can easily prove logically that this is so. However, when spirituality is approached in this fashion alone the destination is nihilism. Because as you slowly realize one concept at a time that the "things" that we took so seriously are in fact just illusions, you begin to see that it can ALL be seen as an illusion. Meaningless. No-thing. This will ultimately, as it did in my case, lead to deep despair and a sense of deep boredom and frustration. It is, in fact, the process of "thinking it through" that is the cage from which one is liberated when this process has finally failed the seeker. The ONLY liberation one can ultimately attain is through the DIRECT EXPERIENCE through the Right Hemisphere of the human brain. Once this is done, simple direct understanding is then used to transcend ALL situations where the left hemispherical world view might formerly assign a "negative" evaluation to a sensation or a perception, thus liberating you from the suffering that accompanies that view. You will be lighter in your approach to life. Liberated from suffering and stress. No external source needed, it's all within you.

10 Enlightenment Commandments

First let me say that I'm not a big fan of the word "Commandment" which implies that I have ANY authority to demand anything from anyone. However, the term is well recognized in this format and therefore continued out of ease. These should really be the 10 Enlightenment "suggestions" but that lacks the symmetry with the form of the original 10 commandments which were meant to be used as a spiritual/religious/philosophical basis for one's life. Likewise I offer these 10 suggestions as a basis for one's path to enlightenment. I hope they serve you. Here they are:

<u>10 ENLIGHTENMENT COMMANDMENTS</u>

1. Accept what is
2. Give kindness without expectations
3. Embrace change
4. Be the change you want to see in the world
5. You are not your thoughts
6. Live without a personal story (there is only the now)
7. For every action there is an equal and opposite reaction
8. Allow no harm to come to others through action or inaction
9. Trust but verify, for those who do not trust cannot be trusted
10. You are the energy that manifests the universe

Explanations:
I will now go over them one by one and give brief explanations for how the suggestions are meant and in some cases why they were chosen.

<u>Commandment 1: Accept what is</u>

Commandment 1 has no reference to God in it and there is a reason for that. The word "God" has become a concept, for some it's an old man with a grey beard sitting on a golden throne in the clouds for others it's Shiva with many arms dancing and yet again for others it's the universe itself. However, since God is greater than any concept that can be held in a human brain and is described in all religions as being "omnipresent" (e.g. – everywhere at once) then there is no need for the word God when by definition God is all that IS. Coupled with this is my favorite definition for the term "love" which is:

Complete acceptance of someone/thing as it is.

When you combine those two concepts you get the simple:

Accept what is

Which is then identical to Christ's:

36 "Teacher, which is the greatest commandment in the Law?"
37 Jesus replied: "'Love the Lord your God with all your heart and with all your soul and with all your mind.' - Matthew 22: 36-37

It however avoids all possible conceptualized versions of the word "God" and the pitfalls that accompany them as well as all the romantic (clinging, desirous, etc.) definitions of the word "love," both of which get in the way of the practice of the commandment.

Commandment 2: Give kindness without expectations

The second commandment is similar to Jesus' as well, Jesus' second commandment was:

Matthew 22 : 39 And the second is like it: 'Love your neighbor as yourself.'

And:

"Do unto others as you would have done to yourself..."

falls into this same category. However, the reason why I didn't use Jesus' "Love thy neighbor" is because of the pitfalls of the word "love" mentioned above. Love is too often mixed up with the romantic version of the concept which is clingy and demanding. The reason I stayed away from "Do unto others" is because there are in fact things that people like done to themselves that others would not enjoy (masochism comes to mind.) So that is why the simple:

Give kindness without expectations was used. Without expectations being of supreme importance because giving with expectations that you will receive ANYTHING in return is egoic and makes the gesture meaningless from a philosophical/spiritual point of view.

Commandment 3: Embrace change

Commandment 3 is not necessary to mention if the first Commandment is followed to the letter, however, as an event, change is worth singling out for spiritual growth. In fact one need only really follow the first and the second commandments by themselves to reach an enlightened state all the rest of the commandments are really for clarification and to highlight certain truths that occur often and when misunderstood or when poorly practiced hinder spiritual/philosophical growth. Within this idea is one of Eckhart Tolle's favorite philosophical points:

"All forms dissolve"

and the reason why I avoided using that term is because forms are often mistaken for material things when the term really means ALL energy forms. Therefore, to avoid confusion about the word form, the more simple:

"Embrace change"

was used. Of course, again, to embrace change, one needs to accept what is.

Commandment 4: Be the change you want to see in the world

Once it's accepted that change is a constant the next phase is to BE the change you want to see in the world. The most effective way to bring positive change is through example. The process by which you can bring liberation to those near you is to first liberate them *from you*. This "changes the rules of the game" and allows them to examine freedom as well. Think about it as if you and your friend or family member were locked in a never ending game of chess, once you stop moving, they have to stop playing as well.

Commandment 5: You are not your thoughts

One of the most liberating moments in the philosophical/spiritual life of a human being is when it is realized that thoughts happen by themselves. They are a natural process like growing hair or breathing and do not define who someone is. So many people fall prey to the constant flow of random thoughts that flow through their heads, and to make matters worse they identify with them. They draw their sense of identity from the random flow of thoughts that cross their minds when the most fundamental examination would reveal that they are not their thoughts because that which notices the thoughts is clearly more fundamentally "you" than the thoughts themselves. Descartes was in error when he said "I think therefore I am" what he missed was that that which noticed the thought preceded the thought. That simple awareness is you.

Commandment 6: Live without a personal story (there is only the now)

This is the only compound commandment and while the two parts complement each other I will explain them both individually. Living without a personal story means to live each moment fresh. Bring nothing to it but your senses. When you approach something or someone don't evaluate them on anything you've experienced in the past. Every time you see someone/thing allow yourself to experience them/it as a newborn baby would. By this I don't mean every time you walk up to a flame place your hand in it, your simple common sense can be used and your experiences of a particular person indeed might be useful but do NOT define the person by them. This applies, even more strongly, to you. The past has no claim on you. Let it go. You are here. Only here. When you think of the past or dream of the future you do so from the present moment. The past and the future are both simply thoughts in the now. There is only the now. Allow your awareness to reside in it and you will be in accordance with the universe and/or God. Remember billions and billions of energy events and particle collisions have happened to create this precious present moment. Honor that by noticing it and you will honor that which created it.

<u>Commandment 7: For every action there is an equal and opposite reaction</u>

This is a general restatement to Newton's third law of motion. It is also often loosely used as a definition of Karma. However, the principle goes deeper than that and also explains why all forms spring from the void in pairs of opposites (e.g. sound and silence, black and white, light and dark, etc.) All motion whether physical or energy based (like in the form of chased thoughts – or rather thoughts with which we identify) creates a ripple effect and goes out into the universe on a path that starts with you. Many people tend to over simplify this and egoically try to classify karma as: "good karma" gives me "good things." This short sighted version of Karma is responsible for many phenomenon's that have been noticed in modern sociological/scientific studies, like when after you feed a poor starving people, something that can be seen as "good karma" or a "good" act, the karmic byproduct of this act is that their population rises. The bad karma that resulted from the "good deed" is then that the people still have no means of feeding themselves or the new children that were created by the karmic action of feeding them in the first place and the next round of starvation is far greater than the original rate. Overpopulation is a huge problem and it can easily be seen that it is a byproduct of many "good" things like greater medical knowledge which leads to longer lifespans, etc. However, in spite of all these "good karmic" discoveries, every 3.6 seconds, someone on this planet dies of hunger. All acts, no matter how noble their purpose, create positives and negatives. Every action creates an opposite reaction and if one turns a blind eye to the negatives they will leave a karmic wake of negativity behind them as they gaze with blinders on at only the "good" they think they are doing. ALL actions should be weighed carefully. The act of removing the ego from actions lessons the overall Karmic impact by a great amount, it does NOT, however, make the karma disappear as some spiritual teachers suggest.

You can understand this phenomenon if you look at it in terms of how one lowers their "Carbon Footprint." You can lower your Carbon Footprint immensely by driving less and using less power in your home etc. and be of great service to the environment. However, every time you exhale you create a small amount of CO_2, and so one's "Carbon Footprint" is never zero while they still have a body. Karma works exactly the same way. So be careful in what you choose to "do" in this life.

This runs contrary to modern man's idea that he/she must be constantly "doing something" or being "productive" however, due to the truth of this suggestion/commandment that impulse needs to be lessened substantially if our species is to survive the next hundred or so years.

Commandment 8: Allow no harm to come to others through action or inaction

This goes beyond the physical, though physical harm is the most obvious form and is therefore already governed by many different society's laws. The part of this commandment that is often never even noticed is in the realm of thoughts and emotions. When one moves about the world in an egoic or Left Hemisphere based mindset they spread a great deal of suffering and pain to others. Then, through the Ripple Effect, the pain and suffering, that emanated from the original person's unguarded thoughts, spreads out and harms others. Buddha said:

"Your worst enemy cannot harm you as much as your own unguarded thoughts."

and while this is true, sadly this harm does not stop with the original thinker. Dr. Jill Bolte Taylor sums this up succinctly when she notes:

"You are responsible for the energy that you bring into a room."

Lastly, the reason why the term "or inaction" was added to this suggestion/commandment is that the willingness to allow others to suffer by doing nothing to stop the suffering is just as damaging as to do the damage yourself. I quote Einstein here:

"The world is a dangerous place to live; not because of the people who are evil, but because of the people who don't do anything about it."

This notion reaches much farther than merely putting a stop to the likes of Adolph Hitler, it reaches into one's own mind when by not taking responsibility for your thoughts, behaviors, and emotions you are, though inaction, not "doing anything" about the amount of pain and suffering you spread to others.

Commandment 9: Trust but verify, for those who do not trust cannot be trusted

Human beings are not alone in the use of verbal deception; the capacity to lie has also been noted in language studies with great apes. Koko, the gorilla made famous for learning American Sign Language was caught lying when after tearing a steel sink from the wall in the middle of a tantrum, she signed to her handlers that her cat did it. It is unclear if this was a joke or a genuine attempt at blaming the kitten, however the idea that the kitten could be blamed at all revealed that the concept of lying or blaming another was within her understanding.

Many deceptive techniques are used throughout nature by animals in the act of mating, hunting, and self preservation. However, humans are alone in the ability to appreciate the harm created by the act of deception. This was noted definitively by Sun Tzu in the Art of War when he said flatly:

"All warfare is based on deception."

This assertion alone is a clear example of the destructive nature of deception and gives an explanation as to why the ninth of the original 10 commandments was:

"Thou shalt not bear false witness..."

The original 9th commandment shares much with this 9th commandment, much of which was taken from a line from Chapter 23 of the Tao Te Ching which read:

"Those who do not trust, cannot be trusted".

The reason for this fact can best be explained by a quote from Thomas Jefferson:

"He who permits himself to tell a lie once, finds it much easier to do it a second and third time, till at length it becomes habitual; he tells lies without attending to it, and truths without the world's believing him. This falsehood of the tongue leads to that of the heart, and in time depraves all its good dispositions."

It is the nature of those who deceive others to mistrust because they are no longer able to trust even their own thoughts.

The reason why "but verify" was added to this is best explained by this insight from the author Stephen King who wrote:

"The trust of the innocent is the liar's most useful tool."

Which creates a paradox here in the act of trusting, and acting on trust, while verifying facts. Trust first, make it your habit, and it will clear your mind of doubts and free you from your own falsehoods. I would like to offer this poem from Sōiku Shigematsu as an example of how this is done:

Deceive me if you will
I'll let you do that
but, I - I'll never,
Never deceive you

You are responsible for only your behavior and by trusting others and always accepting them as they are you free them from any need to lie in the first place.

Commandment 10: You are the energy that manifests the universe

Matter and energy are one and the same. Einstein's theory E=MC2 generally means that the energy that makes up matter is equal to the mass of the matter multiplied by the speed of light squared. That the two are equal. Matter is made up of energy and the amount of it is defined by Einstein's equation. This is a very general explanation of Einstein's theory but for this point will suffice as a clear indicator of the symbiotic relationship between that which we call matter and that which we call energy. And we are all made of it. The same energy and matter that power the stars and galaxies are inside of us and it all sprang from the same "Big Bang" that exploded into existence approximately 14 billion years ago.

We are all made of the same material as the rest of the universe.

There are no separations between any two human beings on this planet. We are all physically connected through a system of energy flow that also extends out into our galaxy and ultimately to the entire universe.

All religions mention in one way or another that God is everywhere, therefore being made from that which is everywhere, we are one with God.

We and the universe are one.

The Most Common "Sins" of Religious Practitioners

First off let me say clearly that this is not an attempt to get anyone to abandon their religious practices or beliefs. In fact It is an attempt to do just the opposite; this is an attempt to encourage people to engage in an actual practice of their religions or beliefs.

In that light let me begin by pointing out the following truths:

Lao Tzu was not a Taoist.
Christ was not a Christian.

Buddha was not a Buddhist.

Muhammad was not Islamic.

Moses was not a Jew (I'm referring to the religion not the race.)

None of these people found their truths, or "enlightenments" as a part of a "group" or religion. They found it individually. In fact, most abandoned their religions to find that truth. Christ was a Jew. Buddha was a Hindu etc.

Why is that do you think?

Am I saying that religions are false? No I'm saying they are FULL of truths that they themselves get in the way of (or rather that their followers commonly miss BECAUSE of how they practice the religion itself.)

The reason why this is so is because the moment something becomes conceptual it loses its true nature. Like saying I am a "Christian" rather than being one who reads the enlightened words of Christ and then lives and practices likewise as an individual. Anything that is a concept IN AND OF ITSELF hinders progress because spiritual truths are non-conceptual. The joining of a spiritual group of ANY KIND (including one that "doesn't close itself to other spiritual groups") can create a whole host of ego-centric and therefore enlightenment-hindering effects. The word "sin" was often used as a translation in spiritual texts for the Greek word "hamartia"

Hamartia (Ancient Greek: ἁμαρτία):

A term developed by Aristotle in his work Poetics. The word hamartia is rooted in the notion of "missing the mark" and covers a broad spectrum that includes accident and mistake, as well as wrongdoing, error, or sin.

Many argue that this isn't how the term would have been understood in Christ's time, but I think that argument is really immaterial. The only question is, is sinning "missing the mark?" I think the link between the concept of religious sinning and Aristotle's word Hamartia are worth noting (and were once interchangeable hence the confusion.) And therefore, if so, what would be the "Sins of Organized Religious Practices?" I would suggest that many organized religious practitioners "miss the mark" by:

Creating "Others" – or "In-Group/Out Group" dynamics *or a "We vs. They" attitude* (all "egos" – false conceptually created ideas of self - need "others" to define themselves against like "I'm a Zen Buddhist, and you're not!")

Irresponsibility – *or an idea that religious leaders are responsible for your spiritual growth* ("My Guru enlightens me..." or "Only my Priest knows the truth")

The Limitations of Language – or the idea that Spirituality can be contained in words (it's a personal, non-verbal experience; words can only point the way, stop reading your holy books and BE them!)

Closed or Completed Truths - the moment you attach a name or title to something you close the concept, you limit it (Like if someone were to say "This is Christianity!" pointing to the New Testament, when anything that Christ would have done as an individual would be a better illustration of "Christianity" than the book or those calling themselves "Christians" in fact, I can see MANY things that Muhammad did, or Gandhi did, or Buddha did, or Lao Tzu, or even Albert Einstein or Albert Camus - an admitted atheist - for that matter did as very "Christ-like" and therefore more "Christian" than people who call themselves "Christian" but don't act like Christ. The proof is in the deed, not the word...)

Spiritual Pride – *or "my belief is the ONLY truth" or "I personally am more spiritual than you"* (I or MY spiritual beliefs are better, or more spiritual, than yours...)

Literalism – or believing in the infallibility of the texts and forgetting that to err is human or more importantly the mistake of trusting "words over experience" (this is a big one, forgetting that man had his hands on these texts and therefore not every word in it can be perfect pointers – words at best "point" to non verbal truths. If Christ or Buddha or Muhammad got their hands on modern books which had their names attached to them it's quite possible that they would begin an immediate rewrite. If something sounds "off" in a spiritual text, it probably is off. Trust the "satguru" or "inner-teacher" in you to know the difference. Truth has a certain "ring" to it and "feels right" in other words it points to and then creates an experience that feels right - like when one hears the phrase "Do unto others as you would have done to you" or Gandhi's "Be the change you want to see in the world" they just "ring true." Judge your spiritual texts by that feeling and you will not go far wrong.)

Creating Time- or "using a method to reach enlightenment" – there is a popular phrase that says "all paths lead to God" and in an ultimate sense, this is true as God is everywhere and therefore there is no way to be "away" from God. However, in Enlightenment terms the phrase should read "all paths (or methods when mistaken for the truth they illuminate) lead away from Enlightenment." The reason for this is that the only place where the Enlightened state can exist without a cloud of thoughts obscuring it, is the perception of the present moment. The Left Hemisphere of the brain needs the concepts of future and past to function, while the Right Hemisphere, the focal point through which the Enlightened state functions, exists here and now. Be here, right now, and be liberated from the world of concepts...

This list isn't all inclusive; don't mistake these words for a complete truth either! This is a partial list of some of the most common "sins" which miss the mark of enlightenment and keep one in an egoic or conceptual world view. This leads to delusion which leads to pain and suffering.

There is truth in most modern religions that will lead you to an enlightened state. Don't "miss the mark" and follow them with your eyes closed, enlightenment is about opening your eyes and waking up to reality AS IT IS.

Now, how about the non-religious "groups?" How about people who call themselves "Atheists." The irony here is that they are, by the very same process, limiting their own philosophical horizons. While most Atheists will claim that they are ONLY opposed to the idea of a "God" they often act, by deed, and therefore in reality, against the entire religion or religions themselves. In these circles much time is spent attacking the religions themselves and not just the singular concept that they claim to have issue with, that being "is there or is there not a supreme being?" Often, of course, Atheists ONLY argue against the Supreme Being that is offered by Judeo-Christian-Islamic faiths and when given a Pantheistic (or in other words "God is everywhere") view they often just shrug and say "so, what's the point of that?" The reason why this concept is lost on them, and on many who have never experienced it (though it's in every spiritual text in one form or another) is that one must have shifted to a Right Hemispherical perception to experience this directly (for those needing a scientific explanation this shift occurs when the Posterior Parietal Gyrus, and the language centers of the brain are reduced substantially in activity.) The drawback to Atheistic practices (as they are lived, not in their theories) are the same as those who cling to one religion as the ONLY source of truth in the universe. It closes one off to reality in the form it takes AS IT IS without concepts layered over it. Also, many Atheists come from an "educated" or "scientific" background that relies heavily on a conceptualized worldview and as such limit themselves heavily to only one hemispherical view (the Left Hemisphere.) The reason why over the years religions have created more enlightened people than science or education is that in religion there is often the practice of "surrendering" oneself (the fake conceptually created "me") to God, this process often leads to the Right Hemispherical shift of perception which leads to the state where one feels "one with God" or "one with all things." This hemispherical shift, we now know from the work and experience of Dr. Jill Bolte Taylor is the very shift that occurs when one enters into an "enlightened" state. Perpetual conceptual thinking (the scientific method and world of "white papers" and "intellectual arguments" etc.) would bar one from entering into that worldview which ultimately leads to the very clear and liberated view that after returning from deep meditation Christ and Buddha and Muhammad all tried to explain, in their own terms, to their followers.

So in the end it's not the title you call yourself, it's the practice by which you live that ultimately defines who and what you are as it happens in the only place where anything can happen, the present moment!

Satsangs
(Q&A With Viewers)

"Satsanga, Satsangam, Satsang
(Sanskrit सत् सङ् ग *sat = true, sanga = company)*

In Indian philosophy *means*
(1) the company of the "highest truth,"
(2) the company of a guru, *or*
(3) company with an assembly of persons who listen to, talk about, and assimilate the truth."

- Wikipedia

I made some videos and received messages in response to them. If you wish to access the videos you can find them at:

www.youtube.com/user/yugcigameht

Here are some of the correspondences between myself and the questioners. Perhaps the answers I give to specific questions will be more illustrative to you. I apologize beforehand for the repetition in my answers, but again, in the end, the process is simple, the application is where people find the difficulty. I hope these speak to you:

Female (Age 21)

Satsang with Female (Age 21) - Letter 1

Dear Mark,

The non-verbal feelings induced by your wonderful channel are difficult to portray via email but I want to thank you so much for helping me to help myself.

At times I have let myself be, shut off the storyteller and therefore felt such wonderful peace but this isn't yet constant. I overanalyze everything (pointlessly I suppose) and I have a couple of questions.

I am a 21 year old woman who wanted to be an Opera Singer and now I seek God, peace, love. Everybody told me I have all it takes to be an Opera Singer (and here my ego is tempted to try and prove this to you, though I recognize it's really irrelevant) but the further my singing progressed, the more my painbody tried to reinforce its perceived reality that I was a failure and as such ultimately unlovable. It had to work really hard. I knew that in singing it is important to keep the tongue free, so my tongue and other parts of the body began to tense up involuntarily. This was both painful and terrifying. I tried at first to ignore the painbody but I still feared it so this often didn't work. When I completely forgot 'myself' (actually I was forgetting the ego and acknowledging the self) and just sang for pleasure it was great but a lot of the time I felt the pain body spreading. The moment I remembered I would identify with it and things got worse. I just about coped with this when I was studying at University (although it was extremely disruptive to my work) because I was socializing often and it was easier to distract myself from constantly analyzing everything. Then I graduated and returned home to live with my parents, little to occupy the storyteller. I had no job and no clear secure 'future' to simulate. I had been busy for most of my life and seldom gave myself room to 'just be'. I reached a sort of crisis point. I would come up with a positive philosophy I and the painbody with its perpetual 'but's and 'What if's would create a new excuse for why I couldn't ever make it as a professional singer/ couldn't ever be happy. I would attempt to meditate and only get more and more agitated 'trying' as my pain body just worked harder until I burst into tears. I recognized that the only true problem was inside myself but I saw this as terrible rather than a blessing.

Now that I know I no longer have to identify with it, it is becoming easier and easier to ignore (even if it sometimes doesn't feel like this is improving whilst I'm in pain-body central). I strive to be honest with myself and am often catching out my ego, seeing it for what its.

I haven't watched all your videos yet so apologies if you have, effectively, already answered my questions.

1) I recognize that the potential to find peace is always there but would you agree that the story teller itself may take a while to heal? Is it sometimes necessary to indulge the problem-solving part of the brain in order to placate it?

2) Although we are essentially one being, I presume we have different mental characteristics?... How do you think this affects our 'true personality' in addition to the development and function of the ego/storyteller/problem solver?

3) Is it possible to live in the present and have goals? The Opera Singer goal is obscuring my view. I hesitate as I realize that desire and expectation are hindrances rather than helpers.

4) Have you any advice on coping with the fact that most people have a different view on how the world works? And many will try to convince me that what I believe isn't real? Or will this just sort itself out? My pain body fears losing this. (As well as thinking I'm a failure, the painbody expects things to fail me)

5) Why do so few people find enlightenment? How/when did this go wrong? Why are so many people suffering?

6) Is the Ego just 'surface chatter'? I'm guessing thoughts in verbal form are the left brain and thoughts that are feelings but not verbal are right brained? Can I control my, sometimes wordless, unpleasant feelings as easily as I can control my verbal thoughts?

Thank you again. You know what it means.

With all my love,

Female (Age 21) xxx

Answer

Dear Female (Age 21),

I was you. It wasn't opera singing it was chess. I understand where you are with this. Ironically there are many people who, in order to "perform" in their arts have come to some amazing insights that they then, sadly, utilize only in their art. I'm not saying that that is or will be you, I'm warning you about being lured into focusing on the singing as "the issue." When you allow your reality, moment to moment, the singing will be solved along with the larger "problems" in one large release. There is no need to tense one's tongue when there is no need to achieve anything

during a performance. Where the performance is no more special than the meal you ate beforehand, or the conversation you had with the person who holds the curtain rope before going on stage, you will see this clearly and no tenseness will remain. If the audience is you, then you sing to you, and in truth you sing to nothing but the beautiful sounds themselves. You as well become a "member of the audience" and enjoy the performance of "that which sings" and it won't be you. I hope that speaks to you ☺

I will move to your questions now:

I recognize that the potential to find peace is always there but would you agree that the story teller itself may take a while to heal? Is It sometimes necessary to indulge the problem-solving part of the brain in order to placate it?

Seeing is the key. There is a paradox here that is also true and that is "It takes time to change one's conditioning, and it can only be done in the now." The entire method has nothing to do with problem solving, it's more akin to a simple watching. When you notice the storyteller beginning to "chatter away" do no more than that. Watch it, don't judge it or analyze it, just watch it. Give it the same energy you would watching anyone/thing perform. Just watch it without being critical or labeling it. This simple energy is that which is in you that holds the world in that way (perception through the Right Hemisphere) and it needs no analysis function. The best way I can describe the process is that in time the storyteller just "stops talking" like someone caught "doing something silly" it just becomes silent.

Although we are essentially one being, I presume we have different mental characteristics?... How do you think this affects our 'true personality' in addition to the development and function of the ego/storyteller/problem solver?

We are one being, and over that is an infinite combination of conditioning that comes from experiences. The conditioning is not you, it's the "conceptual version" of you that includes a "story of me" and various "beliefs and ideas." These beliefs and ideas are often no more than a mixture of your cultural and familial beliefs in one way or another either as positive or negative reflections (i.e. "I'm not like those people in that movie!" or "I'm like my mother in this or that way" etc.) and what we are not exposed to, to us, just doesn't exist. To the universe however, it exists perfectly and functions whether we notice it or not, this is why the closer we become to the manner in which the universe actually functions the less we suffer due to our ignorance.

Is it possible to live in the present and have goals? The Opera Singer goal is obscuring my view. I hesitate as I realize that desire and expectation are hindrances rather than helpers.

Once you embrace the present moment your idea of what a "goal" is will change accordingly. It will change from a fixed point in the future where "something good will happen" to an intention to pursue a path laid before you like a stretch of road. There is a path before you called "opera singer" and there is a step to make on that path, each step is no more important than the next or the previous step and all are along the path. When you sit with friends before the performance it's also part of the Opera Singer path, when you sleep at night, the same. Let go of any ideas about what it is to be an Opera Singer and you will be one, right here, right now, and when in that path it's time to sing you will open your mouth and the song will come out, when it's time to stop singing the silence will fall of itself. And ALL of it is the path, which, more importantly, is not the "role" called "Opera Singer" but is the path of you.

4) Have you any advice on coping with the fact that most people have a different view on how the world works? And many will try to convince me that what I believe isn't real? Or will this just sort itself out? My pain body fears losing this. (As well as thinking I'm a failure, the painbody expects things to fail me)

When you practice the acceptance of everything as it is, no one can "convince" you of anything, including your own thoughts. "What is true?" someone might ask. Your answer will be "that you have just asked me that question." How can anyone/thing convince you that your present experience is anything but what it is? Let go of all worry in this, there is no "state" to achieve, no "great wisdom" to hold more precious than what you are in this moment. What you see, smell, taste, touch, and hear NOW. This IS the truth that cannot be untrue. Within this, there is no fear, there is only the beauty of the universe unfolding before your senses in a private show where there is no right or wrong, there is only what is.

5) Why do so few people find enlightenment? How/when did this go wrong? Why are so many people suffering?

No one can succeed in finding enlightenment because it cannot be lost. The act of living with concepts clouding the present moment is just as valid as living in a way that releases them or sees past them to what is simple and what is true. The egoic worldview is just as valid, it's merely more painful. And because the universe has no "preference" as to how you chose to live your life, you can go about your day with the concepts and the "mental chatter" being in the forefront of your perception if you choose, or not. The failure in the "methods" that are used to bring one to "enlightenment" (which is merely the "lightening" of the conceptual overlay of the universe that you use to navigate in this "body/mind.") are due to the fact that the world view that one brings to the process is convinced of itself. The language centers of the brain have done wonders in convincing you that the stories they've concocted ARE you. And so all teachers are stuck with the fact that in order to transcend this hold it has upon your perception, one has to begin within it. One must engage the language centers of the brain in such a way that they ultimately look past themselves! This isn't easy to do! This is why, great suffering is such a wonderful portal because as my teacher used to say to me "Well, Mark, when you've had enough suffering, you'll probably stop doing that..." (to whatever question I brought to him.) It is conceivable that in the future, through methods like bio-feedback that we can achieve these states at a more rapid pace and in a non verbally based method (meditation is this as well, but many people spend those quiet hours merely conversing with themselves in their heads or succumbing to boredom and falling asleep!) Alas, as of now, we're stuck in this "question and answer" style teaching method, which is right in the heart of the beast! lol. Practice IS spirituality, be present, allow everything that is (not a passive "giving in" to it, but acknowledging, if we don't first acknowledge that a rock is flying at our head, how can we effectively avoid having it hit us?), and trust that the choice you make will be the right one. Listen to that little voice in you that says only one thing usually it's just a gentle "yes" or "no" if you have to convince yourself of anything, be VERY suspect of doing it at all!

6) Is the Ego just 'surface chatter'? I'm guessing thoughts in verbal form are the left brain and thoughts that are feelings but not verbal are right brained? Can I control my, sometimes wordless, unpleasant feelings as easily as I can control my verbal thoughts?

The Ego is a conceptual overlay of thoughts with which we have identified as "me" as opposed to "not me." This includes beliefs brought to us by our experiences and our "story of me." Even with no "spiritual practice" whatsoever your present ego will fall of itself. Do you have the same beliefs you did only a few years ago? I think, when examined, you'll see that this "solid seeming ego" isn't that solid at all! Conceptual thoughts and symbolic language are the playgrounds of the Left Hemisphere. The Right Hemisphere just offers up a subtle and gentle perception of the present moment, and where language is concerned includes subtle cues like body language and tones. Feelings, come from a different source called the "Limbic System" and fear and rage come from a portion of it called the "Amygdala." This is where the bulk of the pain body resides. We have preset patterns in the form of memories and ideas and stories (real or imagined or re-written) that we have stored that we hold as kind of "nightmares" in our "dream of ourselves" that have been triggered so many times that they now no longer need external stimuli to be triggered. For instance, if you have a fear of heights let's say, in time you will not need to be near an edge looking down to have this fear triggered, some other more mundane daily occurrence can be used to stimulate that fear, trigger it, and cause the reaction without any actual heights to be afraid of! We then, by replaying the fearful scenarios in our mind, re-trigger the event over and over and "re-run the loop" and get locked inside the terrifying nightmare. The way out of this is the same method as the liberation from your concepts and that is to allow it fully. When the trigger comes and the feeling occurs ACCEPT IT FULLY. "Ok, I'm having a painbody episode, and that is fine." It only takes 90 seconds for your body to flush out the chemicals that create the painful and uncomfortable state, and only YOU can make it continue by replaying the triggers in your head. Jill Bolte Taylor suggests even counting to 90 if you need to rather than re-triggering the events over and over. And, in the same manner as the ego, by merely noticing these mental events, in time, they will disappear of themselves. Noticing without judgment and allowing completely is the key that unlocks the door to peace in all things.

I thank you for your wonderful questions. Your wonderful light and beautiful soul come through in your writing! Let her out! She's beautiful!

I hope these answers speak to you I wish you peace and grace,

Namaste.

Mark

Female (Age 21) - Letter 2

Mark,

Thanks very much for your last email - although I realize that this is my own personal 'journey' and I should be wary of relying too heavily on others, it is lovely being able to contact you and so comforting just knowing that you exist in the world. Your videos are truly wonderful.

I don't know how busy you are kept replying to emails but I've had a few other thoughts I'd like to share with you in the hope that you can offer some further insight or advise me to drop them.

When in 'painbody central' I find it 'hard' to let go as my ego really has an aversion to presence. It is terrified of failure (or rather, NOT failing), and tries to convince me that I am crazy/losing my grip on reality. I am learning to comfort, rather than berate, myself when I'm feeling low. I trust that I will get used to being more present although I recognize that this will probably be harder at some times than others and I need to be patient with myself. My

SATSANGS (Q&A WITH VIEWERS)

painbody/ego seems to regroup and rebel more forcibly after each 'good' patch. When I allow the painbody fully it tends to induce lots of tears. In the past I thought this was indulging the pain body but perhaps it is necessary. I think I've carried the painbody for much of my life and need to fully accept this but avoid identifying with the painbody by remaining present.

I still find myself falling into the trap of 'seeking enlightenment' in order to 'succeed at singing' but I will persevere in watching this. I keep reminding myself that far more effort is involved in NOT being present (The ego is so very cunning in convincing me otherwise! It is very resourceful and versatile - like a chameleon!).

Thank you for the recommendation - I found Jill Bolte Taylor's book very moving. I am also benefiting from Eckhart Tolle's 'The Power of Now'.

1) If someone is sufficiently present, can the ego part of the brain be 'used' to communicate the energy and compassion of the 'true self' or is it ALWAYS selfish by default?

2) How much is suffering a choice? Am I 'meant' to be suffering when I am or is this simply a case of my not allowing myself to be present? I want to be able to fully trust everything that is and not be discouraged when I have long pain body episodes. (Part of this is fear and guilt about my painbody impinging on others).

3) I'm dubious of this one... the concept of 'evil spirits'. As far as I understand it, evil only exists as is a concept formed by the ego. That evil is simply darkness (lack of light)?

4) Just a curiosity... most of the 'spiritual teachers' I've come across seem to be male - does this ring true to you or is it a misconception of mine? I wondered if it might be because they are more likely to cut through an egocentric society.

With kind wishes and love,

Female (Age 21) xx

Answer

Female (Age 21),

"When the student is ready, the teacher appears..."

Let me first say that there are no "teachers" there are only those that can point to that within you that is already true. That being said, it is the sign that you are serious about this path that draws you to seek answers from a teacher, I did the same and that is why I make my videos and offer myself to the universe where I am needed. My teacher gave to me for over 20 years loving and patient guidance. I am here as you need me in any capacity that takes. There are also many other fine teachers around, but there is an old wisdom about letting the "student find you" and you have found me. I am happy to be at your disposal until you have no further need for me.

The two books you mentioned are going to be a wonderful opening for you. After you finish Jill Bolte Taylor's book read "The Power of Now" by Eckhart Tolle. Jill Bolte Taylor's book needn't be read again cover to cover, just certain sections are necessary for further use (and, in fact, her interview with Oprah will more than suffice as a "study source.") however, "The Power of Now" is meant to be read over and over and used as a weapon against your conditioning as a constant pointer to that which is more primarily you (so, if you need to, and I did this myself, once you finish the last word, crack it back open to page one and start again! Only reward can come from this.)

On the painbody:

"When I allow the painbody fully it tends to induce lots of tears."

When you are in a safe place (i.e. in private or with friends you trust or you will spark a fear response and it will trigger another kind of episode), let the tears flow. Resist nothing and EMBRACE nothing (i.e. don't have a "good cry") let them flow as long as it is a natural flow. The key to this spiritual practice whether in Painbody or in "every day ego" is:

"Whatever you accept completely will take you to peace, including the acceptance that you cannot accept, that you are in resistance." – Eckhart Tolle

If you are feeling sad say to yourself "Oh, I'm feeling sad, and that's ok." Hold it as gently as you would a newborn puppy, don't "squeeze it too tightly" or "hold it casually." Allow it completely and watch it with a gentle, nonjudgmental awareness, and in 90 seconds the chemicals will flush from your body and be gone. This is true of all states even nervousness:

"Oh, I'm feeling nervous, and that's ok." and simply watch the nervousness with the same energy as the puppy and see what happens.

On singing:

Instead of the idea of "seeking enlightenment" at all, it is quite acceptable to use your singing as your spiritual practice, however, keep in mind that what you learn through that practice, has nothing to do with singing, and all to do with life.

And now to your questions:

"If someone is sufficiently present, can the ego part of the brain be 'used' to communicate the energy and compassion of the 'true self' or is it ALWAYS selfish by default?"

The ego and the Left Hemisphere are subtlety different. The ego resides in the Left Hemisphere and is comprised of thoughts, beliefs, and concepts that we have identified with (filled with an idea of "me" or "mine" i.e. "my thoughts" "my beliefs" "my story") It is a product of the language center of the brain and the way in which the Left Hemisphere processes data. However, every mental state includes to some degree or another, both hemispheres, we're really talking about which one is primarily "piloting the ship" and when you shift to a Primary Right Hemispherical view you can still use speech (a Left Hemisphere process) and even solve problems, but you will do it in a non self seeking space. So, the answer to this is that the Left Hemisphere is a wonderful little tool that has mistakenly been given the task of "piloting the ship", when it's better used to highlight little "obstructions" in our path as a search light. As a pilot it's far too narrow a beam of perception to be of use and because of its many "blind spots" we tend to "bump into things" (causing suffering, or "Dukkha" according to the Buddha) when it's lighting our path.

How much is suffering a choice? Am I 'meant' to be suffering when I am or is this simply a case of my not allowing myself to be present? I want to be able to fully trust everything that is and not be discouraged when I have long pain body episodes. (Part of this is fear and guilt about my painbody impinging on others).

Instead of seeing "choice" or "not choice" think of it more like your singing. How much is good singing a choice? Well, once you know how to sing, then the question is more relevant. First practice presence, and then as you do, soon a choice will appear. You will come to an experience in your life and suddenly, where before there was no choice, one will magically appear, like a Y in the road. One choice is to follow the old conditioning and ego, and the other, at the point of "noticing" is a choice to choose to allow it fully, and let it go. In time, as with your singing, there will no longer be effort involved, you will open your throat and out will come beautiful music, similarly, with practice presence will be your default state. Practice IS spirituality. There are many wonderful practices: follow your breath into your body, allow what is fully, feel your inner body, meditation, be in the now, etc. etc. These are all the realm of the Right Hemisphere, if you are practicing within them, the Left Hemisphere can't follow you there!

3) I'm dubious of this one... the concept of 'evil spirits'. As far as I understand it, evil only exists as is a concept formed by the ego. That evil is simply darkness (lack of light)?

Nothing in this universe deserves your love more than the souls that choose to live in the darkness and away from universal love. Their example of suffering is a beacon to show us why the path of the ego, the path of separateness and fear, is painful and empty. Who can say a Demon isn't the greatest of Angels, who has chosen this role to light our way to peace *by showing us how not to be? Give compassion to all who suffer, even the demons of this world. If you come across an evil entity in this world, thank it, and say simply "I don't need your lesson now great spirit, and I thank you for offering it." and let it be, this is with people (though say that in your mind and not out loud to the people) or to any entity you might encounter in this path.*

Just a curiosity... most of the 'spiritual teachers' I've come across seem to be male - does this ring true to you or is it a misconception of mine? I wondered if it might be because they are more likely to cut through an egocentric society.

There are many fine female teachers (in fact Jill Bolte Taylor is one of my primary sources for information) out there, it seems however, that men have traditionally been given this role by cultural bias. Gender is not important in this process (in fact, being female is an advantage! The feminine energy is much more compliant and giving by nature, use it fully!) the ultimate goal is all the same, oneness, which includes us all.

I hope these answers speak to you and if you have further need for my assistance do not hesitate to ask. This is your path, Female (Age 21), however, do not fear to ask for guidance, for that which speaks from within me is merely you, and so you needn't ever fear asking you for advice about you.

I wish you peace and grace.

Namaste,

Mark

Female (Age 21) - Letter 3

Thanks, Mark - that means a lot!

A question I've been avoiding asking you is to do with my living situation.

ANYWHERE BUT HERE

Reality SEEMS to look like this:

I already have large debts from my undergrad and 'need' to save up a large amount for my singing postgrad - this is why I am living with my parents. I will possibly be living with them for many years in order to save up money. Jill Bolte Taylor says that to conserve our own energy we should be careful which people we let into our lives. From a scientific point of view, most of my conditioning has stemmed from my relationship with my parents. My mum suffered from post-natal depression for many years and has a lot of anxiety issues, as do I. This is why, as I recall it, I generally felt a lot more peaceful when I was living at University. My mum isn't entirely adverse to changing our relationship but at times she'll get defensive and say 'look, I'm happy with who I am, it's you we need to focus on improving'. Her 'carer' ego depends on my being happy in order to survive. My 'carer' ego also desperately wants her to be happy in order to survive so there is a clash! When neither of us are present, we often rub each other up the wrong way. My mother thinks that by getting involved in my life she will make me happier but this just feels suffocating rather than helpful. It FEELS like it's harder to keep present when constantly around people about whom the ego has spent 20 years developing conceptions. I am going to suggest my mum reads 'My Stoke of Insight'. I was wondering if you could advise me on staying present in these kinds of surroundings.

I have 'The Power of Now' as an audio file so I will listen to it again and again, practicing being present whilst doing so.

Love,

Female (Age 21) xx

Answer

Dear Female (Age 21),

Conditioning in the form of "roles" is one of the hardest things to break. The role of Mother/Daughter is one that society has created

and has certain expectations about, however, this makes it no less arbitrary and illusory compared to the simple "truth" of the universe. It is still a conceptual overlay over reality as it is. There is a section in "Deceptively Simple" entitled "enlightened relationships" that you might want to revisit that covers this to some degree, and I'll cover it again briefly here.

The key here is to remember that these roles are symbiotic. If both players don't participate, the game cannot be played. Armed with that the key to liberation from this cycle is to stop playing your part. It's like a game of chess, if you stop moving, they can't keep playing. This has the added benefit of allowing the counterpart in this dance to stop dancing themselves, and even, in rare cases to examine the dance and ask "Why am I doing this!?" However, you cannot invest any expectation into this more than what you have control over, and that means you have to release your mother from any expectations about her changing her behavior in any way. Even if she never changes her behavior, that doesn't change one ounce of your job here, and that is to let go of your half of this role. She's welcome to keep "shadow boxing" but that's her path and not yours to dictate.

The key to this, as with all things, is to allow her completely. ANY behavior she exhibits will have to be allowed while you clearly, and with rock solid consistency, with love, enforce your boundaries.

"I love you Mom, and please let me make my own choices here."

As a practice use simple non judgmental awareness.

At first this might be after a conflict or a role has been played out, then you notice it:

"Hmm, I just played my part in a role with my mother…"

Then as your awareness gets better you might catch it mid-role:

"Oh, I'm playing a part in a role with my mother…"

At some point, before you begin any behavior a choice will appear:

"I feel compelled to play a role now with my mother, but I choose not to…"

Ultimately you will come to:

"Oh, here is where I used to play a role with my mother…"

Until finally:

There is no role left to play.

This process is true of all conditioned patterns and is how awareness slowly but surely "re-trains" your behavior, and it all happens by being aware in the now of what is, and accepting it fully without judgment.

Namaste,

Mark

Female (Age 21) - Letter 4

Thank you, Mark.

I had an 'important' question for you last night and I repeated it to myself over an over in an attempt to remember but it's not surfacing. Next time I'll write it down.

I am enjoying using relationships as my spiritual practice and am already noticing significant changes - thank you very much for your explanations of the process!

Before sleep seems to be the most easy time to stay present, as the mind recognizes there is nothing to be done but rest. Your videos really speak to me - they just make perfect sense to me! I watched the '10 Enlightenment

Commandments' two nights ago. As I prepared for sleep my mind began rattling away and parts of my ego kept having what I call 'aha!' moments. I imagine them saying 'We apologize, Miss, we really thought we were working in your favor but now we see clearly we've been laboring under misapprehension!' and bowing to presence. Last night and the night before my mind kept spewing out random fragments - some phrases or words in varying degrees of strength. When it does this it's much easier to recognize that these are not me. I found myself lying in semi-supine and felt my body begin to rock with the vibrations. Sometimes I decide I want to sleep and through this (I suppose it's a form of surrender) the presence seeps in further. Sometimes I feel like it even wakes me (my body) up when I am asleep - is this possible? I've noticed my mind thinking things like 'That's enough presence for today, too much of a good thing.' I hope that each time I notice this thought creep in I'll have more strength to ignore it.

A recurring thought is 'He won't want to read your boring rubbish, he's probably far too busy - stop bothering him!' and I suppose I'm not really sure why I felt the need to tell you all these things, perhaps it is just my ego seeking reassurance and gratification at having 'achieved presence' but I'm sending it anyway. I keep reminding myself how important it is to keep a 'beginners mind'. The other night the thought I kept identifying with is being scared of an evil spirit appearing in my room. Will you comment about Evil Spirits?

Love,

Female (Age 21) xx

Answer

Female (Age 21),

Just before sleep, as you begin to nod off is the easiest time to be completely present, and awaking in the morning is one of the hardest. That's all normal, just allow it fully. Don't let your mind talk you out of peace, it

thinks it's doing it for your own good, and it has good intentions, however the road to hell is paved with...

Feeling the internal body is going to be a new sensation and will stand out at first, in time you will come to feel it as your "normal" state. Just allow the process and don't label it :)

There is no boring rubbish, and there are no "silly" questions.

As far as evil spirits it's important to remember that the highest frequency of energy in the universe is love, all other energies simply can't "digest" it, and anything that thrives on the darkness will not be able to stay around presence. It's simply "inedible" as a frequency to anything that needs darkness, and this will include people as well as anything else that roams this universe. If you sense, or fear anything or anyone, and this is going to sound amazing, but the key is to immediately love it fully. Send it nothing but love and light and if it's truly "evil" it will go away or it will have to, if it remains, raise to the higher frequency (this is true in your relationships with people too, no matter what they give you, if you return love they have to, in time, match the frequency, try it!) Love is the key in all things, fear nothing in this wonderful universe that is ultimately just, you.

Namaste,

Mark

Female (Age 21) - Letter 5

Dear Mark,

I've had two experiences I'd like to share with you.

1) A 'dream' in which I was intensely aware of the energy of my body. It felt like I left my body but was also still in it and I was on my back floating along until I came to a big window and I was supposed to go through it but it was

dark and I couldn't see what was outside so I panicked and wanted to get back to my body/the world of form. This experience taught me just how attached to the world of form 'I' really was.

2) A few nights later I was watching the thinker and the painbody and I managed to use their energy and transform it into light, I was 'sucked' into a presence experience. My eyes closed tightly shut and I think my body went quite rigid. I surrendered and I feel like I reached a 'new depth of presence'. all I can really remember is energy, a sort of slow motion effect and a lot of light. I also felt like something left my body but in hindsight I'm not sure about this.

I don't know what I have experienced and as you said I shouldn't label or grasp on to it these but I wanted to share them with you in case you had any advice to offer. Even if you just say there is no further advice to be given.

Sometimes when I become more present my body seems to screw up... why does this happen? Or is it irrelevant?

It seems that on the nights after I've experienced more presence, I have nightmares - why does this happen?

Is it ok to email you once a week (maximum) IF questions arise? Or once a fortnight? I think if my ego gives itself permission to email you in some sort of regular pattern it'll create less guilt when I feel I want to consult you about things. I'm unsure of the most correct balance between asking for pointers and attempting to deal with it myself. Everytime I start doing 'well' the painbody seems to regroup more forcedly and knocks me back down again. This feels very real but I know it's just thoughts...

Could you please offer some advice about 'Community/Helping others/TRUE selflessness'?

Many thanks, I'm so very grateful for your signposts. Moment by moment, I want to be the best human being I can out of love for God and this beautiful planet.

Much Love,

Female (Age 21) xx

Answer

Dear Female (Age 21),

Never hesitate to contact me when a question arises. Trust your inner voice when you decide that you want to contact me, and let no "schedule" dictate the decision. Have no guilt, all your questions are welcome. It is only, after all, you asking you to point back to you.

Let's examine your questions:

A 'dream' in which I was intensely aware of the energy of my body. It felt like I left my body but was also still in it and I was on my back floating along until I came to a big window and I was supposed to go through it but it was dark and I couldn't see what was outside so I panicked and wanted to get back to my body/the world of form. This experience taught me just how attatched to the world of form 'I' really was.

Sounds like you've answered this one, excellent! Fear nothing in this wonderful universe, follow anything you were meant to see.

2) A few nights later I was watching the thinker and the painbody and I managed to use their energy and transform it into light, I was 'sucked' into a presence experience. My eyes closed tightly shut and I think my body went quite rigid. I surrendered and I feel like I reached a 'new depth of presence'. all I can really remember is energy, a sort of slow motion effect and a lot of light. I also felt like something left my body but in hindsight I'm not sure about this. I don't know what I have experienced and as you said I shouldn't label or grasp on to it these but I wanted to share them with you in case you had any advice to offer. Even if you just say there is no further advice to be given.

Just watch out for the "story" your mind wants to make of it afterward. "I also felt like something left my body but in hindsight I'm not sure about this." No need to know, just to experience. When you let go of knowing, you will experience it fully.

Sometimes when I become more present my body seems to screw up... why does this happen? Or is it irrelevant?

It's only relevant to that which wants to label it as something significant. Let go of that and be present, let no stories or ideas tell you how or why to be, just be. Present standing. Present walking. Present crying. Present in the fetal position. All are just the same.

It seems that on the nights after I've experienced more presence, I have nightmares - why does this happen?

This is very normal. As you begin to dent the Pain Body it becomes "very clever." It starts to look for ways "in" and sees your sleeping state as a WONDERFUL place to have "free reign" over your mind. Let it. It's the sign that it's losing the game and becoming desperate. The future will hold all kinds of "impulsive wild emotional thoughts" that arise with no stimuli to "catch you unaware" and then when those stop working, it will just send "fear" or "anger" down the line to see if It can "snare" you into attaching a memory to it and beginning a "loop." Just smile at all these antics, they are the antics of a desperate mental construct that fears its own demise. When you wake from a nightmare after a day of peace, that means you're doing PERFECTLY. They won't last forever, but it's all a part of the process. Wake and say "Thank you pain body for doing what you think is best for me, I have no need of it anymore." and go about your day.

Could you please offer some advice about 'Community/Helping others/ TRUE selflessness'?

I know this answer will be unsatisfactory at present, but the answer is work on yourself, that's the best gift you have to give the world. Once you do that and make progress, events will simply "show themselves" to you and you will know it was meant for you to be helpful in that moment. Some young lady might e-mail you with questions, or even more probable, some friend will be in a position to hear about the things you've learned, and when they are finally "ready" you will be there, speaking not as a guru, but from direct experience, about your own life and what you've learned and it will open the door for their awakening. Never push this on those not ready to hear, you often only get one chance to get this message through, and if they don't want to hear it, they won't and you will miss an opportunity later when they are ready, because they'll dismiss it at that point as "Oh, that enlightenment crap! You already told me about that, now how about my boyfriend!?" or something. Keep this jewel to yourself and share it with your kindness and your compassion and your example as a person. Give wisdom ONLY to those ready to hear it, or it will be wasted, or worse, twisted for egoic purposes.

I hope these answers point to that which you need to see.

Question any time, and if there is need for a longer discussion, we could use Skype. You do seem to be making wonderful progress, trust it fully. Keep reading "The Power of Now" and doing your inner work.

Spirituality IS practice.

Namaste,

Mark

Female (Age 21) - Letter 6

Dear Mark,

I've just watched this video

http://www.youtube.com/watch?xxxxxxxxxxxxx&feature=related

I wasn't sure what to 'think' and I wondered if you had any advice to offer in connection with its content, delivery or with the views of its author, Mxx Xxxx.

SATSANGS (Q&A WITH VIEWERS)

I found the following view online:

'When a Buddhist realizes Enlightenment... The "Great Compassion" cannot but arise in his or her heart. He is no longer able to view the world in the same way he did before his Enlightenment. He can now see, feel, know, and understand... If one person is sick, hungry, homeless, or dying in the world... There is a part of him that is sick, hungry, homeless, or dying. He no longer feels separate and safe. He views the world as a sea of suffering and is directly connected to each and every suffering being, in the same way the ocean connects to each and every wave.

*It's really a choice all Buddhist practitioners make... To change themselves in a way that is of benefit to all living beings, and not just their 'Self.' This transformation is founded on the direct experience of "Enlightenment" in Mahayana Buddhism. The path that leads to "Enlightenment" is called the 'Path of the *Bodhisattva.'*

Reconnecting to the world in this very special way, does not end the Bodhisattva's suffering, however... In some ways Bodhisattva's may suffer more, but each time they help end the suffering of another being, their suffering is also eased.'

Could you address particularly the part I've highlighted? My thoughts are that if I lived in an enlightened state, suffering would still be experienced but would be 'bearable' because I would know that the suffering was NOT me in my essence? Is it 'true' to say that the real end of suffering cannot fully be realized until no creature is suffering? Love is the highest frequency and suffering cannot survive where there is Love.. so does the planet 'need' to be totally consumed by Love for the final end of all suffering? How does Nirvana fit into this? My mind suddenly feels TOTALLY out of its depth. It suspects there is an infiniteness to this which it will never truly be able to grasp. Am I getting too bogged down with theory?

At times I have been tempted to abandon my life situation completely but I suppose doing so wouldn't actually help me to achieve anything because it's what's happening inside that counts... Have you any comments to make regarding alcohol, caffeine and other substances? How might they affect my ability to access presence? What about diet?

If you'd find speaking over skype more convenient than replying via email my skype name is Xxxxxxx.

Love,

Female (Age 21) xx

Answer

Female (Age 21),

The film is a propaganda campaign for a cause. The way to make effective propaganda is to start off your piece with little bits of "truth" and then move toward the "big conclusions" by adding to the end of the bits of truth some grand and forcefully spoken "known quantity" that simply can't be known.

For instance:

"God seen as an entity has this and this drawback, while God seen as no entity has this and this drawback"

Taken from a thousand different theological debates in man's history (literally thousands of philosophical books on this subject), and from these insightful works, which might be new to the viewer, the speaker sounds "deep" and therefore as if they are speaking from an "enlightened source" and then, at the end, they throw in what they want to pitch as "truth"

"God isn't.. blah blah blah, God is ACTUALLY... blah blah blah"

No human has the capacity to know this. It's beyond our form limitations. ANYONE selling you on their certainty about such things is either delusional or lying with the intent of swaying you to their authority.

"The current government is corrupt and there are people hoarding wealth..."

known and obvious truth...

"Therefore there must be an evil group of people who are in CONTROL..."

This is simply the ego wanting an excuse not to do the work by creating "others" to blame. The problem with ANY person put in a position of power is that they haven't done the internal work and still function from an egoic space. From that egoic space, no matter how noble their purpose, they will create problems, because they can't function from a space of "oneness" and therefore won't solve issues in a way that doesn't create separation. The problem isn't some "group of illuminati" the problem is a genetic weakness that we've bred into reality through choosing our mates with more aggressive characteristics and over time morphing man through natural selection into an aggressive, self centered, and greedy creature (you're a young woman, ask yourself what characteristics in men – assuming you're heterosexual - do you seem to naturally prefer, and if you do you might see this.) So, no matter WHO they are, unless they have first done the internal work necessary to get a hold of that "beast", they will continue to foster that behavior externally through their internal wiring, NO MATTER THEIR INTENTION TO DO OTHERWISE. There is no one to blame but evolution, and there is no solution except for everyone to do the work, one person at a time. I'm sorry love, there is no "movement" that is going to bring an end to this through pointing fingers at "the bad guys" and then by just getting rid of the "bad guys" everything is perfect. The new people who take the place of the old will end up just as corrupted and lost because they haven't done the work. The work is the only solution I've ever found that has a chance to take care of this problem. And it's done one person at a time. Don't join a group, fix Female (Age 21)! ☺

He then goes onto talk about the fact that there have been civilizations with the same level of technology as ours that just vanished, etc... This is again, pure hypothesis, not fact (as he asserts with great conviction.) If they invented plastic ALONE there would be TONS of it still left lying about... Nonetheless, the REAL point is, that THIS GUY WASN'T AROUND SO HOW CAN HE SPEAK WITH CERTAINTY ABOUT IT?

It's just certainty being sold to sway people. If someone walks up to you with certainty about "how things actually are" beyond their small little space of experience and self knowledge RUN don't walk away from this person!

Certainty is the drug that is sold by propagandists. It's the ultimate con-game and it's what the Left Hemisphere longs for above all other things, a simple answer that it can call its "own" and hold forth as "true."

There is no certainty about the nature of "everything" that man can ever have.

So, the key to this, is to accept uncertainty fully. Alan Watts wrote a great book about that called "The Wisdom of Insecurity" and it's worth reading.

The Right Hemisphere through feeling at one with the energy of the universe doesn't need certainty in the form of some "story" or "in group/out group" philosophies that foster a feeling of the "superior" we verses the "inferior" they. This is all egoic worldview and quite destructive. If you hear anyone talking about "the they" I'd be VERY suspicious of what this person is talking about, because that's the egoic worldview.

After the beginning he gets into how "it's all consciousness" and we are "thoughts from God" etc. which is just his new interpretations of Hindu and Buddhist dogmas and nothing new under the sun.

The sole reason why I'm neither a Hindu or a Buddhist (or any ist or ism) is because on top of the wonderful practices that they've created to generate inner peace, which I do ascribe to, they then offer this entire mysticism of certainty about their particular religious beliefs (reincarnation, multiple

Gods and Goddesses, etc. etc. etc.) and NONE of these are important to the practice itself and ALL of them are certainties beyond the capacity for humans. The purpose of these mythologies is to sell certainty to a mass audience who, without the divine authority that certainty implies (I mean, who but God could tell you what is certainly true? Well if these guys know certainty, then God must have chosen them, etc..) to sway them into joining the group/religion (like the guy in the video you showed me) The truth is that none of that is needed to find a deep inner peace, I, for instance, only recommend the practices of the religions, not the mythologies (Watch my video on miracles to see some of how I mean this.)

I know this is a lot to absorb and the Skype conversation might be necessary to have this conversation fully so you can give feedback that is tailored to your needs in understanding this extremely complicated subject matter. It's probably not going to be handled well in this form, but I hope this gives you something to chew upon as feedback from the video.

This situation won't get fixed by groups, it will only get better one by one. Work on Female (Age 21), and be an example of love and truth for others, and the universe will give you opportunity to teach that to others. Trust me! Don't rush this! Work on Female (Age 21) first! You have a big heart and want to help the world, but you've gotta start at home and your home is you.

Now onto your other questions...

"Reconnecting to the world in this very special way, does not end the Bodhisattva's suffering, however... In some ways Bodhisattva's may suffer more,"

The point of all this isn't an end to all suffering, the point is an end to self created suffering. You will always, if you have a heart, feel the pain of others. And that is a wonderful practice, compassion is the way we touch others. It's like pain in the body. Pain is the body's way of warning you that there might be danger in the form of tissue damage. It's a wonderful thing, and suffering comes from resisting the pain. Fear is another one, it's a warning that there might be danger in the environment and starts a sub-routine to look for potential danger. Wonderful, thank it fully. Not all conditions the mind labels as suffering are in fact suffering, suffering is the act of generating needless resistance to what is. The rest just comes from having a body and needing to protect it to maintain the form.

"Love is the highest frequency and suffering cannot survive where there is Love.. so does the planet 'need' to be totally consumed by Love for the final end of all suffering?"

Love is the essential nature of all things, suffering comes from not seeing it clearly. Nothing more. What we refuse to see through denial, is the love that the universe has brought forth in this present moment. It's always love, we only label it otherwise through thinking.

"How does Nirvana fit into this?"

Nirvana as a mystical state of perfection simply doesn't exist (unless you let go of all form, it's the default state of all energy, e.g. love.) No need to chase it. Enlightenment is the consistent and vigilant "lightening" of one's conceptual overlay to reality. The state of Nirvana is usually ascribed to a degree of proficiency with this that makes for VERY rare moments where conceptual reality skews our perception. Living in that is a very blissful and peaceful place that generates a felt sense of oneness. That space, is Nirvana, at least in the human form, as close as we're going to get.

"Have you any comments to make regarding alcohol, caffeine and other substances? How might they affect my ability to access presence? What about diet?"

All drugs effect the function of the brain. Alcohol for instance either stuns or outright kills brain cells when it enters the bloodstream and gets to the brain. The "stunned" cells cease to function and therefore the brain centers that are hit the least get a chance to "come out and play" etc. NONE of this is necessary to achieve bliss or peace. Caffeine increases brain activity and if you are having trouble maintaining presence, it will be a tremendous problem (the dominant Left Hemisphere will demand more "things" to fill it up for instance.) After you gain some mastery this problem will diminish substantially (Eckhart Tolle still drinks Coffee from time to time, I also ingest caffeine, but I only re-started after obtaining a large degree of *mastery in right-hemispherical perception.) Diet and exercise will be excellent at bringing one's body to a better functioning state and that health will help the process, however, other than the drugs, you can be completely unhealthy physically and have a perfectly peaceful and blissful state. I would suggest, in the short term, letting go of drugs of all kinds, also puzzle solving, like crosswords or games like chess. They can also be "drugs" for the Left Hemisphere and will cause problems in the practice early on.*

"Am I getting too bogged down with theory?"

Yes. Theory is the food the Left Hemisphere wants you to consume, so you stay away from practice, which is what it fears the most. The ego wants to hijack spirituality and make it a "conceptual thing" where it can maintain control. Let go of all theory and practice, spirituality IS practice, nothing else matters.

Let me know if or when you wish to Skype and we will set it up.

Peace and Grace to you love.

Namaste,

Mark

Female (Age 21) - Letter 7

Dear Mark,

Many thanks for your detailed response!

I mistrusted the video for the following reasons:

1) Its apparent fear-inspiring intentions

2) The bold statements it makes with absolutely no 'proof' or reasonsing

ANYWHERE BUT HERE

3) The 'Them vs Us' mentality it projects

4) The unpleasant defensive nature of its author

5) Its failure to highlight the importance of the now and practising awareness,

6) The unfeeling way in which its author utters the words 'I Love you all'.

However, I wondered if there were aspects of truth in it - the comments about chemicals in water and substances that may affect our ability to access presence? I suspected as much about caffeine and alcohol - I will avoid them completely from now on! Do you have any further suggestions to make regarding diet? Or any sources to recommend? I now understand that I don't 'need' to abandon my life situation, but I am concerned with adjusting it to help me access presence more easily (perhaps this is the wrong way round... and the ego is expecting salvation in the future once I have the correct diet etc, but I still feel this knowledge might be useful?).

'However, other than the drugs, you can be completely unhealthy physically and have a perfectly peaceful and blissful state.' - I had been curious about this as Eckhart Tolle really does have the most appalling posture, ha! Thank you for this knowledge.

Thank you for the recommendation of Alan Watts' book - I may read it but as the simple phrase 'The Wisdom of Insecurity' already resonates with me, for now I think it might be best if I avoid theoretical research, just keep listening to 'The Power of Now' and practising awareness. Although, I suddenly just thought - 'The wisdom of insecurity' and 'Trust but verify' seem to contradict each other- can you explain this? Perhaps I should get the book after all!

Your comments on Suffering, Nirvana and Love were also very helpful - thank you!!

Thank you soo much I'm very grateful for your pointers!

Much Love,

Female (Age 21) xx

SATSANGS (Q&A WITH VIEWERS)

Answer

Female (Age 21),

Much of the dietary suggestions I might make are all fairly well known and more for physical health. Follow known truths for your personal health reasons, but as for presence only practice will help you in this endeavor (people who are on their deathbeds, in the worst possible health, are capable of the most amazing present moments, even with no training) this is a practice that does indeed seem to be beyond the body. That being said, nothing wrong with being healthy for health's sake, but for spiritual health it's completely unnecessary (Eckhart has bad posture, even the Buddha was a jolly fat man - as am I, however I seem to be losing a lot of weight with no effort, it's bizzare - while many people in AMAZING physical shape are complete messes as human beings.) Try to not look at anyone's exterior in this process, it's a very dangerous practice. The mind sees physical health as a sign of mental health (it's a mating impulse) but the two things are simply not absolutely connected.

The Wisdom of Insecurity deals with the fact that we will never know certainty. Trust but verify also comes from the same place, in other words, it's better to trust with no evidence WHATSOEVER another human (complete uncertainty) than to mistrust everyone and everything. However, we are capable of simple awareness with another person, and if they show signs of selfishness, greed, etc., we are not bound, as spiritual people, to just continue to put our head in the lion's mouth. Verify through simple, non aggressive, awareness that comes from a loving place. But, like a child who misbehaves, we can show this person love, and not continue to allow them to harm us. The same is true with "universal truths" trust that this universe is here to love you, and then verify it through observation. There are dangers to our form in this universe, and we have been given this wonderful tool of the Left Hemisphere to separate us and to inspect other "forms" for potential danger. This is the "but verify" half of the brain. Buddha's middle way shows us a path of the spiritual while embracing the form. Trust (spiritual) but verify (honoring form.) We have come to use little of the first, and too much of the second, but, think of it like an injured leg that forces one to limp for awhile, once the injured leg becomes stronger the objective is to return to a balanced gate, not to then go so far as to create a limp favoring the other leg.

Yes, keep with your practice of the Power of Now and your internal work. Your "spotting" of the motives of the film maker come from a state that shows a greater degree of presence in your life. An enlightened swordsman named Tesshu was frequently asked by his students:

"It's like you're reading my mind! How do you do that!?"

and he said (paraphrasing)

"It's not hard to notice the ripples in someone else's pool, when you don't have any..."

The point being, as you continue down this road, and your mental "attachments" decrease you will begin to notice immediately where others are "attached" with little effort (think of it like meeting someone who's REALLY into something that you have had no exposure or interest in, it's pretty obvious that they are a fanatic as they focus energy on it and talk about it often, in time, much of what people find as a "normal" degree of interest in things will seem like an inordinate amount of interest in "nothing special" to you. And you will seem like a mind reader to those around you who still cling to attachments to the world of form. It's not mind reading, it's just that your pool of the mind will have less ripples and therefore be more like a mirror, and will easily reflect the image of the universe as it is, in time, this will lesson your need to "but verify" as your internal feelings about people and the world at large will become much more attuned to the nature of the universe.)

As always, it is my pleasure and honor to point to the truth inside of you.

Namaste,

Mark

SATSANGS (Q&A WITH VIEWERS)

Female (Age 21) - Letter 8

Dear Mark,

I understand that I can only really work on myself, and that I need to let go of any expectations about improving others, but could you please read the following scenario and offer me advice accordingly?

This morning I was having a discussion with my mum and then she started moaning because three people had sent her Christmas cards to whom she had sent none. I tried to gently offer advice and she got really cross. So what is the best way around this? I'm assuming that simply agreeing with her and offering sympathy in this way is not a good idea because it just encourages the 'feeling guilty' ego. Do you think that, in general, just remaining silent is the best policy at these times? My family's collective ego is totally governed by fear and guilt. Often conversations at the dinner table go from discussing one person's problem (often somebody outside of the family whose problem we can do absolutely nothing about) to the next person's problem and so on and so forth! So is it best to either stay silent or remove myself from the situation if possible? I don't want to isolate myself or be passive agressive but I suppose it's a good idea to protect myself from unnecessary negative energy?

She is still angry - does this mean that the advice resonated with her and the ego is reacting against this? She said something like 'I'm sixty four years old now, I don't need to address any issues - I've been through all that and I'm happy with how I am!'

Although she just said this, in the past she has taken mine/somebody else's advice and recognised that there are parts of her that she's willing to change.

So, because I live with her, is it always worth attempting to give the advice? Or just taking each situation as it comes and, through presence, feeling which is most appropriate (offer advice, remain silent or remove myself)?

Love,

Female (Age 21) xx

Answer

Dear Female (Age 21),

Yes, her ego is threatened and she has yet to identify it as the problem. All egos have defense mechanisms, and when you discuss their core issues they usually revert to anger because you are threatening the denial mechanisms that keep them going. As tough as it will be, neither silence or advice is the path, it's compassion. Just listen with compassion and love and wait for direct questions. They have to ask direct questions and then the rule I give to my students is never to discuss "spiritual theory" but always to speak from personal experience, for instance:

Instead of: "You know Mom, there is no ego, there is only awareness..."

It would be: "I've recently found that I have a lot of behaviors that are conditioned that don't serve me..."

Put your own head in the noose and then be willing to be open and vulnerable as you expose what you've learned, even in the face of scorn or ridicule. Your response to their ego's attacks against your new knowledge will be a HUGE doorway for them (if you stop dancing, they will have to as well...)

But this must ONLY come from direct questions like:

"I don't know what to do Female (Age 21), what do you think I should do?"

or

"You seem so much more calm, what are you doing that changed you?"

etc.

These moments are rare and they should not be squandered by trying to force information through a closed door. These questions are cracks in the door, and that is when you can gently place some wisdom inside. Until then, just sit and send them love, no matter what they are doing. They are lost and in the dark, they need the light of your love.

As far as where you should live, by all means find a place where you can be around people who live in the light, but you will find in time they are hard to find. You must be your own light, and many many will notice and ask you these questions, where you must be willing to be open and vulnerable if you want to reach past their egos to their true selves.

I hope this serves you, but before I go I will quote Gandhi:

"Be the change you want to see in the world."

Namaste,

Mark

Female (Age 21) - Letter 9

Thank you so much, Mark.

I've been watching this video:

http://www.youtube.com/watch?v=XBGlF7-MPFI

At first my ego mistrusted Marshall Rosenberg but I decided to keep watching and have really benefited from what he has to say. It has helped me to properly understand what you said about compassion.

I've realized that, so far, in sending you emails, my ego has been trying to seek reassurance from you that I am 'doing well' on my path. This realization has been extremely liberating to me - now I feel I can ask you questions freely, without trying to impress you. I've noticed that if I am struggling to achieve presence it is because I'm letting certain thoughts trip me up. So, when this happens, I want to let you be the light that shines through the fog so that I can see my path clearly.

Thoughts that have been tripping me up are

- 'I only 'deserve' peace in moderation'

- 'I will be happy if I can help someone else achieve happiness.'

- 'Life would be boring if I was present all the time'

- 'Progress (in general, and specifically here regarding right-hemispheric perception) is impossible'

- 'I'm failing at achieving presence'

On the surface I realize the absurdity of all these thoughts but clearly I don't deep down or I wouldn't still be identifying with them. Can you please offer some advice?

A couple of weeks ago I started sleeping with someone and I now realize 'the relationship' was feeding my ego. I first started sleeping with him purely out of lust but then I thought that building a relationship with him could work because we had been good friends for years and he is open-minded, empathetic and creative. However, when I spoke to him about it last night he said 'I don't feel for you beyond friendship'. I'm glad I spoke to him about it early on because now I am ready and able to go back to a purely platonic relationship. From this experience I have learnt to be a lot more reserved sexually - it seems to me that women, as bearers of children, just aren't built for 'casual' sex. Do you have any advice to offer on building these kinds of relationships? I realize that I don't 'need' a relationship but would like to feel better equipped next time a potential 'love interest' crops up.

Ever grateful and with much Love,

Female (Age 21)

Answer

Female (Age 21),

On the video:

I watched the first 21 minutes of this just before he began his method and I like it. He is describing life in (and communication through) the Left Hemisphere (good/bad - right/wrong – superior/inferior – should/shouldn't, etc.) and we as a culture have come to embrace this, because, as he said, in peaceful loving cultures they don't behave that way. Unfortunately to the victor go the spoils, and the aggressive cultures that have taken over this planet now get to have the karmic backlash of their aggressive programming, and that is, that when there are no more external enemies to punish, in order to maintain the aggressive practices, you have to feed upon your own people, or yourself.

So, ultimately, the shift from Left to Right Hemisphere (when one abides in the Self, or in the Right Hemisphere, these behaviors will just seem silly and won't happen) will solve this problem by itself, however, and I haven't watched the rest of this video yet (though I intend to) I'm sure from his opening discussion that his methods will be fine.

Now to other questions:

"I've realized that, so far, in sending you emails, my ego has been trying to seek reassurance from you that I am 'doing well' on my path. This realization has been extremely liberating to me - now I feel I can ask you questions freely, without trying to impress you."

Wonderful! And, more importantly, the very fact that you exist impresses me! No need to try in the least.

"I've noticed that if I am struggling to achieve presence it is because I'm letting certain thoughts trip me up. So, when this happens, I want to let you be the light that shines through the fog so that I can see my path clearly."

Wonderful, I have recently written a short description of the "behavior re-wiring process" and I will share it with you:

Unraveling a conditioned behavior

When practicing ridding oneself of a behavior that one has noticed through awareness, it's important to be patient and non-judgmental (if you judge yourself you just add suffering on top of a process that needs none to work perfectly.)

My experience of this is that the entire process is handled with simple awareness. Accepting what is, then watching it with non-judgmental viewing. It's important to remember that this takes time, it doesn't go away immediately. There is a process and a progression which I would like to share from my experience and it goes as follows:

1. You are completely unaware of the process

2. You notice the process in hindsight (well after the event has passed)

3. You notice the process JUST after finishing (shaking your head wondering why...)

4. You notice the process mid way through it and have the option of stopping it in the middle of the process and dropping it

5. You notice the process JUST before it begins and a Y appears in the road offering you a choice of going down the same old road, or choosing another path.

6. You notice the triggers for the process as they show up and the feelings begin to stir, and you let go of them immediately

7. You notice the build up to the triggers and are completely prepared for the situation and let go before ANYTHING arises

8. The process disappears from your life completely.

This is the progression so never fear, it takes time and patience to re-wire. The tool with which we accomplish this is through simple non-judgmental (Right Hemisphere based) awareness and then your natural intelligence will do the rest (through observation the brain will re-value it all on its own.)

If the behavior includes a partner, then once you are out of the loop, your partner will have no one to dance with, and will have the option of re-examining the behavior themselves and one of two things will happen:

1. They will be unsatisfied and look for another partner to continue the dynamic

2. They will be released from it as well and follow you to freedom.

So fear not! You are doing well on the path! It takes time to re-wire, or to learn a new behavior (in this case presence) so don't despair and don't let your Left Hemisphere should or shouldn't you into feeling like you're failing in this. It takes time to become present, and the only way is to be in the now! (A wonderful paradox!)

Now let's look at your thoughts:

"'I only 'deserve' peace in moderation"

The "I" that says this is a self created fantasy, peace IS you. It's your default state of existence.

"I will be happy if I can help someone else achieve happiness."

This is a deflection that the Left Hemisphere offers up to keep you from looking at what terrifies it, at itself. Now ask yourself, what REAL thing would be afraid of being examined?

"Life would be boring if I was present all the time"

Boredom is the sensation of your Left Hemisphere not getting enough stimuli. In fact the ONLY way to be bored is in the primary Left Hemisphere perception. The Right Hemisphere doesn't need external stimulus to feel perfectly at ease peaceful, even blissful. ONLY the Left Hemisphere experiences boredom.

"Progress (in general, and specifically here regarding right-hemispheric perception) is impossible & "I'm failing at achieving presence"

The process explained above will destroy these ploys to get you to embrace the "there's nothing to do" trap that the Left Hemisphere would LOVE you to embrace. I mean, if there is nothing to do, you will get more of the same, right!? Don't fall into this trap, it's a long way out, here is another recent essay I wrote on it:

The "I've Solved the Riddle of Awareness" Trap

There is a huge snare in this process that can hold you captive for many years (I know it held me for close to 20 years) and the process is as follows:

1. I feel like an individual in a sea of "others"

2. There are moments when I don't feel so "lonely"

3. Someone introduces me to the concept of "non-duality"

4. I examine it and see, through arguments based in Determinism (http://en.wikipedia.org/wiki/Determinism*) that we have no free will in the ultimate sense, because all the particles that make up our bodies and the*

energy that flows through us are just extensions of the motion created by the Big Bang that were headed on this course on a pre-determined path and will continue long after we're gone on the path it was meant to travel, and all decisions we make were meant to happen and only we can fill them with a sense that we made them... etc.

5. Satisfied with this the mind (Left Hemisphere) thinks it's got it "all figured out" and uses this as a pat answer to abide in a nihilistic state of "What does it matter!? It's all pre-destined anyway, so no matter what choice I make, it's what I was meant to make, so bring in the dancing girls and put the champagne on ice!"

6. Anytime anyone suggests they examine their own behavior, they bring out the "smoking gun" of "Who is there to examine this behavior!?" or "To consciousness it's all one anyway" etc.

7. As a result of this we continue as egoic self-centered people and generate suffering for ourselves and others behind the shield of "If you suffer, even by my hand, you were meant to suffer!" (This would have been a great argument to fuel the Nazi's by the way!) And go about our merry ways generating karmic explosions wherever we go, smug in our self-righteous certainty that we've "got it all figured out..."

Well, when, as my teacher used to say "You've had enough suffering from this" (missing that if you generate suffering through ego-centricity, since we're all one, you generate it for yourself too!!) you get to a place where you are depressed and now you're in a meaningless pre-determined universe in a sea of self created suffering...

And it's hell, let me tell you, it's a hell I don't wish on anyone or anything...

So, what's been missed!? What's been missed in this is the old warning not to use fire to burn fire. Not to use the mind to transcend the mind. This "seeing" has to be taken from the head to the heart. It has to be something brought into your experience, and from this experience, you will laugh at how simple your explanation was. How narrow a vision it was and you will be released from it. But it MUST be seen from a different point of view (through the perception of the Right Hemisphere) to be seen in its entirety and then ultimately, when the laughter ceases from how funny it is to watch the Left Hemisphere in its certainty, you will open to an entirely NEW universe, where determinism is only a small part of the play (like the difference between Newtonian Universe – determinism – and the Einsteinian Universe - Relativity.) It's an eye opening thing to see, and from this relative view you can either see the universe as deterministic, OR a completely free place to create in the present moment through intentions that lead us on a ride that's a wonderful (full of wonder) place to be! Joy fills your heart and you don't just LABEL others as "part of the one" you KNOW from direct experience that they are, and you lose all desires to harm, berate, or feel superior to them because it is just a silly notion to harm oneself. Not because of any "concept" you have about the "oneness" of things, but by the same process that you wouldn't harm your own body... You love your neighbor as yourself in mind, body, spirit, and deed, not just with your thoughts.

Now, lastly I would like to share with you another essay I've written about techniques to enter into the Right Hemisphere:

How To Enter the Right Hemisphere

The method by which we "step to the right of the Left Hemisphere" is to engage the external and internal stimulus that the Right Hemisphere is designed to perceive. As it turns out, most meditative practices are meant to do just this.

1. Soften your vision (or close your eyes if you are too distracted by visual "labeling" at first)

2. Feel and listen to your internal body

3. Stay very alert, but don't attach the alertness to any concept or object

4. Don't follow mental stories or labels, just allow them, in fact the act of just "observing them" without labeling them (often called Observation Meditation) is simply the Right Hemisphere examining the

Left Hemisphere and is the act by which the bulk of meditation is practiced.

5. If you want to play sound or music when you do this, the music should be without lyrics to decrease the impact on the language center. If you throw in nature sounds (birds chirping, water flowing, waves crashing, etc.) the Right Hemisphere will be engaged UNLESS you begin to single out and label any of the sounds.

6. Boredom as a sensation means you're making progress, and the Left Hemisphere is not getting enough stimuli, this is where most people trip up and can go no further, because DEEP boredom feels like a kind of "death." And in fact, it is a form of death, it's the Left Hemisphere losing blood flow by being de-prioritized, and since we hold our sense of "self" in there when we begin this process, it will feel as if the "YOU" as you perceive yourself to be at this moment, will start to fade. In order to stop this function the Left Hemisphere will shoot "fear" into the system (fear is a state where we see ourselves as separate and it's a way to keep us in our Left-Hemisphere identified state) which is meant to "shock you" back into its clutches. In time you will see it coming and by allowing it fully, get past it.

7. This "sending fear" technique will be a constant attempt by the Left Hemisphere as you continue to master this process, allow it fully and in time it will actually be funny to watch as it tries to "trick you" into identifying with it, but ask it a question "If you are so real, why do you need tricks for me to see you?" It doesn't like that question and has no answer...

This is a good start for those interested. I can't say how this compares with meditation techniques that others use, this is what I use throughout the day (sometimes I sit and 'formally meditate' but in time, this can be done anywhere and anytime.

On relationships:

Before we get to effective relationships it is first important to see ineffective relationships for that I'll defer to Eckhart Tolle's excellent video on this subject:

ANYWHERE BUT HERE

http://www.youtube.com/watch?v=V3miuaOWsj8

Begin there and we will move forward from that understanding.

You're a young lady and hormones are going to be powerful, don't mistake hormone impulses for YOUR impulses either, they are just hormonal impulses. Don't place identity in them.

This is quite a bit of homework to handle and it should give you a bit to do. Please do the work! It's the only way to progress (though you seem to be doing so, it's my job to keep saying it! lol)

Namaste,

Mark

Female (Age 21) - Letter 10

Thank you!

Haha, ego said 'Of course I'll do the work!!!' and was desperate to impress you by doing the work. Then I noticed this and laughed!

I'm glad you said that about hormones because one of the things my ego sometimes attaches itself to is 'I enjoy sex more than other people'.

I've seen that video before - thank you. Knowing that the painbody really has nothing to do with the person at all is such a relief! Could you please elaborate on feeling whether or not to begin building a relationship with someone? I think I understand what to do when already in the relationship, as I've heard about this from Eckhart Tolle.

The "I've Solved the Riddle of Awareness" Trap *sounds horrific! This is why I'm so determined never to forget the phrase 'The Wisdom of Insecurity'.*

SATSANGS (Q&A WITH VIEWERS)

Re Unraveling a conditioned behavior: I think I may have mentioned this before but often my throat muscles tense up (to do with singing) and at times I let this trip me up... I suppose it is just a kind of specialized painbody and can be dealt with in the same way?

Today I had extremely painful menstrual cramps and I didn't take painkillers because I wanted to use it for enlightenment. However, the pain was VERY intense (causing me to be sick a number of times) and I wasn't brave enough to fully go into the pain so sandwiched myself between two hot-water-bottles. I think I also was trying too hard to 'use it for enlightenment'. Next time this happens do you recommend I abstain from taking painkillers or not? The cramps can last up to about 5 hours.

I'll keep going with the practices.

Much Love and gratitude,

Female (Age 21) xx

Answer

Female (Age 21),

On relationships and sex:

You are a young woman, sex and relationships will happen, the drawback is escaping into them or becoming egoically attached to them.

Sex is an act of intimacy with another human being, focus on the other human being, be there with them, not inside your internal sexual experience and this too can be a spiritual practice.

Remember, that your job in a relationship is to accept your partner fully, NOT TO CHANGE THEM! You are NOT in a relationship with someone to enlighten them. You are not in a relationship with someone to teach

them. You have one and only one job and that is to accept them fully. Love them even when they don't "deserve it" (this does NOT mean put up with abuse of any kind however!) and support them fully as themselves. IF and I mean IF the subject matter of "enlightenment" comes up BY THEIR REQUEST you are to discuss the subject matter from your personal experience as we talked about before. If not, then remember you are dating an egoic person, and that was your choice, so accept that fully. If you find yourself mentally judging them for being egoic, then YOU are failing in your job to accept them as they are fully. This will be a tough spiritual practice, but who doesn't deserve your love fully?

Your other questions:

"I think I may have mentioned this before but often my throat muscles tense up (to do with singing) and at times I let this trip me up... I suppose it is just a kind of specialized painbody and can be dealt with in the same way?"

Notice it and let go of the labels. No longer label it as "tensing", just notice what it feels like. Just notice it without judging or labeling it and in time you will go through all the steps I mentioned before and the behavior will disappear. These words like "nervous" or "tensing" are often self fulfilling because of the label given to them and the emotional energy implied by the label, they are just internal sensations, not worth resisting at all. Just notice them and if the body has no need of it it will let go all on its own.

On physical pain and enlightenment

There is no need to challenge yourself by resisting physical pain or cold or any other extreme conditions to see if you're "enlightened" let go of that desire it's a mental construct. If you find yourself in pain then allow the pain completely. If you find yourself in a menstrual cycle then take Advil or whatever you need to lessen the pain. It proves nothing to "suffer through it" except that you weren't wise enough to take Advil ☺ If the natural flow of your life puts you into a situation where allowing a painful or uncomfortable situation is called for, accepting it fully is all you *need, there is no need to "train yourself" to do this. Let go of any goals to "become" anything, and be here now. Accepting what is here and now IS enlightenment, there is no need to seek out any external situations to "test" what is here and now, it already is.*

You are doing so well, very few people at your age are as dedicated to what is, you will be fine, be in no hurry, you are already far ahead of the game.

Namaste,

Mark

Female (Age 21) - Letter 11

Dear Mark,

Thank you very much for inviting me to join the 'Xxxxx Xxxxxx' group! :-)

I have been working to identify my most potent 'attachments', both negative and positive. In yellow I have highlighted the ones that I still find myself identifying with.

Negative:

UNLOVABLE/REJECTED

Weird/freak/embarrassing

Clingy

'I' can't 'connect' with anyone but sometimes if I feel I AM connecting with someone I feel the need for sexual intimacy with them. Then if they are seen to be an 'inappropriate' sexual interest and they show signs of finding me sexually attractive then I begin to fear them.

ANYWHERE BUT HERE

More specifically - FAILURE

Imperfect/not 'good' enough

Unreliable

Bad singer

Young/naive/ignorant/unimportant/weak

Unintelligent

General failure/things are getting worse

Positive:

NEED FOR APPROVAL/ENCOURAGEMENT FROM SOMEONE ELSE

Empathetic

Reliable

Committed

Mature/powerful

Beautiful

Sexually alluring/'good' at sex

Friendly/easy going/helpful

Ill (needing care)

More specifically - SUCCESS

Intelligent/articulate

Funny/fun

Need for closure/to get everything on the list done

Healthy– good posture, energetic

Alive/sensitive

Good singer

SATSANGS (Q&A WITH VIEWERS)

Original

Creative

Carefree/relaxed

Need to 'improve'

Need to be free of attachments (ha!)

Need to be present

Having written these I found it interesting to note how some of the 'attachments' are registered as something to do with 'me' whereas others just relate to experiences; ultimately they ALL just relate to experiences! I've realized that some of the positive attachments have been created to counteract the negative ones.

You might not feel there is anything to say in response, I just wanted to share this with you. Now my ego fears you rejecting me!! It thinks If I email you too frequently/send you something irrelevant you'll get irritated by me.

Much love,

Female (Age 21) xx

Answer

Dear Female (Age 21),

The first and most important step is to see. Just see. Notice the attachments and then let them pass. Notice any underlying "feelings" that go along with the attachments. How does "Not good enough" feel in your body? What does that sensation feel like without any label attached to it? What does it feel like when the thought "Bad or Good Singer" comes up? What feeling is attached to the concept? Notice it. And do so for the others. Watch for subtle judgments that get attached to concepts and feelings like "This feeling is bad" or "This feeling is good" or "This feeling

is dirty" etc. When it comes up, look at that judgment too. What does "bad" feel like? What does "Good" feel like? etc. If a memory comes up as you do this just notice it too.

Just notice and your natural intelligence will take care of "the work."

You are welcome for the invitation to Xxxxx Xxxxx. Cxxxxxx is a great person and there are many fine folks in that group. This does not mean that everything that is stated in that group is something that I would personally agree with or suggest as a useful practice. It's up to you to "feel" your way through any material given to you and trust your inner voice. If you want my opinion, of course I will give it, but your internal voice is the one that knows your own path regardless of anything I (or anyone else) suggest.

You are doing quite well, keep it up!

Let me know if you need or wish to chat and we'll Skype again otherwise I look forward to your next correspondence.

Namaste,

Mark

Male (Age 23)

Satsang with Male (Age 23)- Letter 1

Hi there,

My name is Male (Age 23) and I just watched your video On Suicide. The last week or so I have been obsessed with listening to Alan Watts on YouTube and just stumbled upon your video by seeing it on the side bar while listening to Alan Watts.

The timing is quite good as I've been suicidal for a while and it is particularity sharp this past while. Like you were, I don't seem to connect with others, at least in ways that are authentic and meaningful, and this holiday season I lost one of my best friends. So I'm feeling sorry for myself, I guess.

But the point is I'd would love to talk with you as getting to bottom of what I truly am is all that matters to me. I just can only seem to understand it abstractly through my intellect and don't know how to...merge or be whole again.

I don't even know you but I feel we have so much in common, and it would be a relief to hear from someone that there isn't something wrong with me.

Please let me know what you think,

Male (Age 23)

Answer

Dear Male (Age 23),

First off I want to say that there are two realities of depression, one is the cause of it (which is the wiring of your brain) and the other is the reality of it on a daily basis (which is the chemicals in your brain causing the suffering.) If the reality of it is overwhelming and places you into a state where you are unable to function, then as a short term solution some medication would be in order. You have to make this call for yourself, it's not a form of weakness or sickness, it's a result of wiring that has been reinforced through behavior and is now out of sync with its intended function (and you're not alone in this!!!!)

The next step is to re-wire that conditioned behavior, and the beginning of this process is to SEE the process.

I'd like you to obtain two books if you are able, and the reason for this is that with multiple sources pointing to the same place, sometimes one voice says something in such a way that another might not and it "hits home" more effectively. This is not to say that that person is then "your guru" it's important during the beginning of this process to SEE clearly. Alan Watts is excellent in this, but I'd like to add two other sources here for this process that will be more directly related to your specific condition:

"The Power of Now" by Eckhart Tolle

and

"My Stroke of Insight" by Dr. Jill Bolte Taylor

With Alan, Eckhart, Jill, and myself all giving you the same material (but from subtly different angles) it's bound to get through and begin the process of SEEING this conditioned perception as it is, and re-wiring it to where it was meant to be.

"The Power of Now" is going to be your primary re-wiring tool, and it will need to be reread multiple times as Eckhart Tolle's sole purpose in that book was to AWAKEN people from your very condition (as your condition is EXACTLY where he started on this journey.)

"My Stroke of Insight" will be the beginning of your understanding on the scientific level, of what is actually causing your pain and suffering and will open you up to the worlds of the two hemisphere's of your brain, one of which, is out of control and causing you great suffering.

In the interim I want you to watch "Deceptively Simple" many times, as there is a lot of material in it and one viewing won't allow it to settle in (in fact feel free to use it as a break from reading) also Videos by Alan Watts (he has some great books too but they are for after seeing the initial reality) and then ultimately Adyashanti (another good one for after seeing the initial reality) will come into play. I'm going to give you some meditation techniques in the short term, but you will have trouble performing them as your condition will preclude and sabotage the process, however, KEEP AT IT, and be brave enough to fight through the resistance and it will help you in this process:

How To Enter the Right Hemisphere

The method by which we "step to the right of the Left Hemisphere" is to engage the external and internal stimulus that the Right Hemisphere is designed to perceive. As it turns out, most meditative practices are meant to do just this.

1. Soften your vision (or close your eyes if you are too distracted by visual "labeling" at first)

2. Feel and listen to your internal body

3. Stay very alert, but don't attach the alertness to any concept or object

4. Don't follow mental stories or labels, just allow them, in fact the act of just "observing them" without labeling them (often called Observation Meditation) is simply the Right Hemisphere examining the Left Hemisphere and is the act by which the bulk of meditation is practiced.

5. If you want to play sound or music when you do this, the music should be without lyrics to decrease the impact on the language center. If you throw in nature sounds (birds chirping, water flowing, waves crashing, etc.) the Right Hemisphere will be engaged UNLESS you begin to single out and label any of the sounds.

6. Boredom as a sensation means you're making progress, and the Left Hemisphere is not getting enough stimuli, this is where most people trip

up and can go no further, because DEEP boredom feels like a kind of "death." And in fact, it is a form of death, it's the Left Hemisphere losing blood flow by being de-prioritized, and since we hold our sense of "self" in there when we begin this process, it will feel as if the "YOU" as you perceive yourself to be at this moment, will start to fade. In order to stop this function the Left Hemisphere will shoot "fear" into the system (fear is a state where we see ourselves as separate and it's a way to keep us in our Left-Hemisphere identified state) which is meant to "shock you" back into its clutches. In time you will see it coming and by allowing it fully, get past it.

7. This "sending fear" technique will be a constant attempt by the Left Hemisphere as you continue to master this process, allow it fully and in time it will actually be funny to watch as it tries to "trick you" into identifying with it, but ask it a question "If you are so real, why do you need tricks for me to see you?" It doesn't like that question and has no answer...

This is a good start for those interested. I can't say how this compares with meditation techniques that others use, this is what I use throughout the day (sometimes I sit and 'formally meditate' but in time, this can be done anywhere and anytime.

I know this might seem overwhelming, but it's too important for half measures, so you have my full attention my friend. I was there. I remember what it was like. There is no more lonely feeling in the world, and I'm here to tell you you're not alone. There are many wonderful people who are here to talk you through this and help lead you out of the darkness. But, YOU have to make the steps. YOU have to do the work, because if not you will merely get more of the same. And as my teacher used to ask me "So, Mark, how is that working for you?" LOL Yeah, I know I felt the same way when he said it...

Male (Age 23)right here, right now, is where you are. It's where you will always be, and it's beautiful, wondrous, and YOU. It's past time for you to meet you.

SATSANGS (Q&A WITH VIEWERS)

All my love my friend, and if you need to talk to me personally we can Skype, but if you don't do the work, I can't help you and would not be serving you if I fostered that behavior. Please get those books and begin the process of seeing YOU.

Namaste,

Mark

Male (Age 23)- Letter 2

Mark,

Thanks for your quick and thorough reply! Yes, I think we should talk on skype as I'd like to ask you some questions that may lead to more questions, and because I'm actually quite knowledgeable of this work (I've read power of now and a new earth dozens of times, meditated for years, did yoga, etc), so I'm definitely missing something vital or have belief that's getting in the way.

My handle on skype is xxxxxxx

Thank you so much for your attention,

Male (Age 23)

Answer

Male (Age 23),

Ok will do. Give me a date and time and we will Skype. I would like you to get Dr. Taylor's book before we do and read it (it's a pretty short book) so we have a common reference for dialogue. You might be stuck in the conceptualization of the nondual philosophy (I was stuck in that for years) her book will give you a "real world" target for release and peace (the Right Hemisphere.) For me, knowing that there was something concrete to achieve, helped me immensely, maybe it will for you as well.

Please let me know when or if you have finished the book and we'll Skype with the information freshly in your mind.

There is a way out, we just have to get past the "igniting fire with fire" phase (using the same tool to get out of the darkness that creates the darkness...) and once this is achieved it will be an easy portal out of the darkness to follow that light.

Namaste,

Mark

Male (Age 23)- Letter 3

--My Letter After Skype Conversation--

Dear Male (Age 23),

It was a pleasure chatting with you yesterday. I want to remind you that now that you've got an idea what's going on in the brain that the original nondual material will make more sense when you read it (you'll know what they're talking about better than they did! lol) So if you can't find Jill Bolte Taylor's material, please go back and re-read "The Power Of Now" by Eckhart Tolle (the present moment is one place where the Left Hemisphere can't function, it simply can't follow you here to torment you if you are present. When he talks about ego, he means "Left Hemisphere" when he talks about thoughts he means the brain chatter generated in the Left Hemisphere, etc. - if you want neuroscience translations for any of his other terms, let me know...)

I will see what I can do about Skyping you tonight or tomorrow (chaotic here!) to check up on you and see how it's kicking in.

http://www.oprah.com/oprahradio/Jill-Bolte-Taylor-on-Oprahs-Soul-Series-Video

http://www.ted.com/talks/jill_bolte_taylor_s_powerful_stroke_of_insight.html

http://www.ted.com/talks/iain_mcgilchrist_the_divided_brain.html

Here are some videos for you to peruse this should give you some homework before we chat next :)

Don't you dare give up:

"No one gets to their heaven without a fight" - Neil Peart

Namaste,

Mark

Male (Age 23)- Letter 4

Mark,

Thanks Mark! I can't express how much your individual attention means to me right now (literally, as I can't seem to feel much). I feel quite selfish but it really seems to make me feel better.

Tonight would be great, but tomorrow is Okay too - whatever works for you.

I am a bit hesitant to read The Power of Now again as I've been exposing myself to his teachings for a while to the point where it has lost its effects on me due to memory covering up the message...but I will.

I meditated for a couple of hours last night, just trying to witness everything. I noticed:

My mind and body are in rough shape...there are tired and foggy. I'm scared I can't function anymore or that I'm going to be disabled

eyes kept focusing repeatedly after soften gaze.

I've been so passive for so long, just sitting seems to make me worse as thoughts get stronger

Thought patterns are so ingrained that they can almost "play" unnoticed.

Fell asleep once

Fear didn't seem to surface (but it did this morning)

forgot I was even meditating numerous times (which is scary as I feel I have ADD and chronic fatigue at the same time) - it is almost like I've burnt so much energy thinking that there's none left, then starts again when I do, just to quickly burn out again.

Talk soon,

Male (Age 23)

Answer

Male (Age 23),

Don't fear the Power of Now, even if you read it and nothing comes, the words themselves will be doing wonderful things to fight against the darkness (the entire book is an assault against the Left Hemisphere...) In fact read it and try NOT to understand it. Just watch the words go by and

let it kind of "flow" into you. Don't concentrate or speculate at all. Of course when you get a hold of Jill's book, feel free to switch.

There is no need to do this "all at once" in a formal meditation style. Throughout your day, pause and notice your thoughts. If you are sitting and formally meditating and you are unable to continue, stand up, move around. Go for a walk and watch as your mind identifies the surroundings and labels and categorizes everything. The key now is just to watch the thing work without actually "doing" anything. From your description sounds like you made a good effort. Just remember to bring the observations with you during your day, just pause, even if it's for a few seconds, and just notice. Just watch your thoughts, your perceptions, the sights, sounds, feelings on the skin, etc. Simple observation many times during your day is even better than formal meditation, the combination of both even better.

Try not to label ANYTHING you see in any way (not even "I'm tired" or "sad" or "sluggish" or anything, instead of the label feel how tired feels in the body, how sad feels, etc.) just observe.

I will try to Skype you tonight (Saturday) and we'll have a brief chat.

All my love my friend, the darkness never lasts forever!

Namaste,

Mark

Male (Age 23)- Letter 5

Hi Mark,

No worries. I am sorry - I was out for New Years unexpectedly. Monday should be good - I'll be on skype then!

Today, while sitting with my eyes closed (keeping vision soft is very hard for me), I felt uncomfortable as it seemed to take work to maintain upright posture...but after a while I did start to feel settled and calmer and in better mood than normal. I also noticed just how much I am thinking and how tense my breathing is.

At a party, I noticed how everyone (especially my age) is so...crazy... not in the traditional sense, but so uneasy and all over the place - their eyes were constantly scanning for something or someone better than the situation they were in or the person they were with. I have to admit, I did the same...there was something sad and disturbing about how a bunch of people gathered to connect yet only on a very thin, almost dead, level.

I hope your new year's went well,

Male (Age 23)

Answer

Male (Age 23),

The world of the Left Hemisphere is dead. It's all certain concepts. Certainty kills life, it strangles it and places it into a rigid category (my favorite quote about certainty is: "Only the closed mind is certain...") I'm so glad to hear you felt a moment's peace, there is SO much more where that came from my friend.

Keep looking around, at your own thoughts and behaviors when you get a moment, and at how never satisfied people are who are locked into this "search mode" always looking outwardly at a world of "objects" that are "other than" themselves.

You will make it to the light, and then you will be a beacon for others, so get ready, when we're done here it will be your turn (as this is mine for you!)

Fear not! lol It's not that bad a job!

All my love my friend, namaste,

Mark

Male (Age 23)- Letter 6

Mark,

it seems the world we created perpetuates this way of living (through the left). It seems so pervasive - and there are few people who I can talk about it with. In fact, language itself doesn't do it justice so it's impossible to explain to anyone what I'm trying to do.

well, we'll see how it goes. I'm really looking forward to talking tomorrow!

Male (Age 23)

Answer

I'll Skype you at 7pm PST if there's an issue with this time (I have to check with my "boss" - e.g. girlfriend to see if we had something planned) I'll let you know.

And yes, the world that western man has created is a dead one, but those living in it are not! In time you will be the light that brings them out of darkness. That is the definition of the word "guru" by the way (not the etymology, just the popular usage) "One who brings light to darkness."

You are on your way to becoming one as you release the light from within you into this deadened, conceptualized, mechanized, outwardly focused (how many people prefer to watch t.v. about other people's fictional lives rather than live their own!?), and certain world we've created.

I will talk to you tonight if all goes well, good luck with your job. Remember a job is just another moment, it's not a means to an end, it is just what it is.

Namaste,

Mark

Male (Age 23)- Letter 7

Mark,

the practice is not going so well - the practice between "accepting everything" and my breathing work seems to be conflicting because if I accept what is, I have no reason to do anything, including the breathing work, which requires me to force myself to do it despite not wanting to. And that's the whole problem - I don't want to do anything anymore. I can't seem to surrender fully, because if I did, I wouldn't have a problem doing anything either, would I?

My other teacher, Mr. Xxxxx, is, from my perspective, getting tired of me and is quite brutal - he doesn't give much sympathy and thinks I'm manipulative. I am manipulative - I'm so selfish and numb I don't seem to think in terms of others, despite being deeply bothered by others "not caring." It's quite confusing because he seems awakened, but isn't very compassionate.

I'm a bit drunk at the moment, so please forgive me if I'm a bit crude.

I'm also confused because you feel like more of a teacher because you are always there, but he seems so confident and has evidence I can't question behind him.

SATSANGS (Q&A WITH VIEWERS)

I'm still ruminating about my cousin and my family - so deeply hurt that we can't just express our love instead of trying to win arguments. She just sent me fb messages instead of actually talking to me and seems so objective instead of compassionate. I've been crying the last day or so a lot but it doesn't seem to make things better.

Answer

Male (Age 23),

Don't confuse acceptance with resignation. Accept doesn't have a negative feeling to it. If you accept what is, it is easy to then "do things" because that is the beginning of effective action. For instance if you accept that the breath work IS needed then it is from that acceptance that you will do the work. The key there is to notice that all resistance to it is simply the mind (Left Hemisphere) making stories about what it wants or doesn't want (positive or negative evaluation functions.) IF the work IS necessary then let no mental or physical sensation talk you out of it. When a sensation (pain, boredom, etc.) comes while doing the breathing work, accept it, and move on. When a negative memory comes accept it, DON'T WALLOW IN IT. Accept the memory and any emotions it stirs IN THE MOMENT, don't swim in it and tell "poor me" stories about it. You will find that the mind wants to constantly sell you that it's "doing what you ask of it" but it's subtlety sabotaging it. It turns acceptance into resignation, it turns love into clinging, it turns the now into movies about the past or projections about the future and most of these movies are "problematic" movies that need some kind of "solution" and of course, the mind is right there to offer you those solutions (because it has been conditioned that problem solving is a high priority function, and it has been for years!) And what are the solutions it conjures recently? It's main one is killing yourself... What a wonderful tool to listen to...

It's time that you let go of all your stories, even the stories that you ARE doing the work...

Just sit and do. Allow everything in the moment but DON'T CHASE IT. Allow then RELEASE it.

What you resist persists.

There is another shore, but it takes effort to get there. Effort that can only be done IN THIS MOMENT and not in your head...

Namaste,

Mark

Male (Age 23) - Letter 8

Mark,

thanks again for being there for me! I just reread your email, and your fb post again as I'm more alert right now.

It makes sense to me and feels right to accept what arises but not feed the stories or assign negative/ positive meanings.

The whole pain-is-payment-for-pleasure/love/good is really helping me as before I only focused on the end of pleasure and the continuation of pain - now I realize that there will be pleasure again as long as I keep paying for by allowing it fully and therefore by allowing the reciprocal downside. It also makes me realize more just how manipulative I am and how I want others to be different from who/what they are (my cousin's decisions, family, etc.)

The breathing work is making me confident that I will be able to function and take care of myself again. It is was more painful to not receive family support when also feeling that I can't handle the reality of my situation. That said, my experiences have still impacted me and left a a deep rooted sense of fear - I'm just realizing how fragile we all are.

I know you've told me many times already it's possible, but it's still hard to stay motivated to just sit in my hostel room and feel the sensations from the present moment. It's unreal how much crap comes up or how much discomfort which seems to make me move before I know I'm even doing it. So far, only watching the breath has given me brief moments of peace. How long did this take for you again and for how many hours a day approximately did you do this lol?

I'm feeling fairly stupid because I can't remember what you said half the time - you were about to tell me last night why you think that is? Even writing emails is difficult you lol. It's almost like there really is nothing to say but I'm confused and want to express myself at the same time.

I'll keep practicing,

Male (Age 23)

Answer

Male (Age 23),

It makes sense to me and feels right to accept what arises but not feed the stories or assign negative/ positive meanings.

The whole pain-is-payment-for-pleasure/love/good is really helping me as before I only focused on the end of pleasure and the continuation of pain - now I realize that there will be pleasure again as long as I keep paying for by allowing it fully and therefore by allowing the reciprocal downside. It also makes me realize more just how manipulative I am and how I want others to be different from who/what they are (my cousin's decisions, family, etc.)

This insight proves you're doing fine. The work of being here now, and allowing all thoughts to arise without following them or making them into a story is about creating space between you and the thoughts. In that space you are able to separate yourself from them and see them. That process leads to insights like the ones above. You're doing the work, those insights show it. Without the space even if I had spoken these truths to you you would not have been impacted by them. They would have been dismissed, with the space, the presence that comes from doing the observation meditation work and inner body work you are now able to see these truths about yourself from a safe distance, and then the next step is to remember that they are just conditioned mental patterns, they are not YOU.

The work, breathing AND observation meditation and inner body meditation give you space, a gap, a distance between you and the thoughts so that your natural intelligence - Right Hemisphere - can inspect them and see them as they are. The Right Hemisphere is the only thing that CAN perceive things as "new" and so gain "insight" out of thoughts and patterns that have been repeated many times with certain Left Hemisphere evaluations attached to them. The insight breaks the certainty which breaks the hold on you.

The irony of this work is it's like a good film director, when they do their job at their best, you should not even notice them. The work is the same, its job is to create space, and so since we can't perceive that space except in terms of freedom (or for you "relief") then it seems like it's not there, but that's a Left Hemisphere world view (the Left Hemisphere wants tangible, graspable, evaluate-able items or it doesn't even "believe" in them.)

You are doing the work, fear not. those two statements prove it.

Namaste,

Mark

SATSANGS (Q&A WITH VIEWERS)

Male (Age 23)- Letter 9

Hey Mark,

just wanted to check in. I hope everything is going well with you. I read all your fb posts but don't feel driven to participate at this time.

I've been doing the breathing work to the best of my ability (but make lots of mistakes; eating, oversleeping, ruminating, getting emotional all cause hyperventilation and keep me from resetting my respiratory center - which naturally wants to stay where it is or maintain homeostasis).

The good news is is that after watching my breath and then reducing it repeatedly, it suddenly relaxed and lessened on its own (far more than I could make it do so with willpower!) and then I felt like falling slowly inside a void and was more peaceful than I ever remember being. I even got up to go to bed and the feeling stayed with me as I lay down, but rumination began to creep in and I awoke like I always do the next day. I'm a bit more motivated now, though.

I also noticed from doing the work this morning and then eating around 1pm, that food really makes it hard to be sensitive to the present moment (at least for me - it numbs me out and makes me tired). I think I'll try eating lighter and only when I'm hungry.

What were your blocks when practicing? Did you feel back pain, tired, rumination, urges to consume food and drink? Did you avoid these unless you absolutely needed something? My biggest challenges seem to be not meditating itself but giving into food, sleep, masturbation (with objectified ladies in my mind's eye), rumination, poor posture - all stimulation that causes hyperventilation - when I'm taking a break.

Also, I noticed that the Buddha did not mention anywhere about giving the present moment priority as a meditation. So far I have only found anapana-

sati as a foundational practice. I'm not challenging you, I'm just feel accepting what is not working in the sense that I can't seem to do it lol.

Let me know how you are doing and what you think about all this,

Male (Age 23)

Answer

Male (Age 23),

The Buddha called himself Tathagata (one who comes and goes thusly) which means that he had no attachments to past or future. It was the central core of his worldview and behavior.

The breathwork is a wonderful practice and notice that the focus of the breath is only possible in this present moment and it is also only monitored by the Right Hemisphere! So, walah you're there!

There are many many practices that will bring you into the domain of the Right Hemsiphere we talked about breathwork when we first started speaking, there are many many other paths as well, but it's working finally so WONDERFUL!

The main hurdles in the process of my recovery were rumination (incessant story telling function), suffering due to depression and a lack of gratitude for what I had, a strong suicidal drive, and waking back into the former painful states no matter how much work I had done the previous day. Those were my biggest obstacles but no two people are alike in any way even their depression!!

You are making progress all around it seems! The breathwork is giving you access to your more peaceful circuitry (Right Hemisphere) and your accepting what is (accepting that what you have lost was worth the pain, etc...) is aligning your perspective so that your Left Hemisphere need not ruminate *as much about it because when you accept something it's no longer a "problem" that needs "solving." No problem, no evaluation, no stories to tell, in short no need for those painful and incessant Left Hemisphere practices.*

Keep it up!! You're making wonderful progress. Just watch out for all this evaluation of the progress with positive or negative evaluations because your Left Hemisphere desperately wants to hijack this whole thing and turn it into a "problem" it's "solving" with a method that it can now call it's "own." etc... This process leads to rigidity, don't follow it. Do your practice. Be your practice, but don't make it an identity, your practice is not YOU any more than your depression was.

Wonderful news my friend, you are well on your way, but then again you have been for awhile now!

Namaste,

Mark

Male (Age 23)- Letter 10

Male (Age 23)'s answer to my previous e-mail was the italicized sections below:

Male (Age 23),

The Buddha called himself Tathagata (one who comes and goes thusly) which means that he had no attachments to past or future. It was the central core of his worldview and behavior.

Right.

The breathwork is a wonderful practice and notice that the focus of the breath is only possible in this present moment and it is also only monitored by the Right Hemisphere! So, walah you're there!

:)

There are many many practices that will bring you into the domain of the Right Hemsiphere we talked about breathwork when we first started speaking, there are many many other paths as well, but it's working finally so WONDERFUL!

I can't seem to get back there for the last 24 hours lol - It's quite frustrating.

The main hurdles in the process of my recovery were rumination (incessant story telling function), suffering due to depression and a lack of gratitude for what I had, a strong suicidal drive, and waking back into the former painful states no matter how much work I had done the previous day. Those were my biggest obstacles but no two people are alike in any way even their depression!!

Those seem to be the same in nature as mine...did you find your whole personality/mood change as you reached the evening? How did you eventually wake up consistently feeling normal or did it just "happen." I'm finding myself unmotivated - I'm just doing this because I know no other escape - so being consistent is impossible.

You are making progress all around it seems! The breathwork is giving you access to your more peaceful circuitry (Right Hemisphere) and your accepting what is (accepting that what you have lost was worth the pain, etc...) is aligning your perspective so that your Left Hemisphere need not ruminate as much about it because when you accept something it's no longer a "problem" that needs "solving." No problem, no evaluation, no stories to tell, in short no need for those painful and incessant Left Hemisphere practices.

Keep it up!! You're making wonderful progress. Just watch out for all this evaluation of the progress with positive or negative evaluations because your Left Hemisphere desperately wants to hijack this whole thing and turn it into a "problem" it's "solving" with a method that it can now call it's "own." etc... This process leads to rigidity, don't follow it. Do your practice. Be your practice, but don't make it an identity, your practice is not YOU any more than your depression was.

Wonderful news my friend, you are well on your way, but then again you have been for awhile now!

Namaste,

Mark

Answer

Male (Age 23),

did you find your whole personality/mood change as you reached the evening?

I did find that my moods shifted profoundly during the day (getting lighter toward the evening), however I spent most of my day saturating my brain with talks by Eckhart Tolle, Adyashanti, Dr. Jill Bolte Taylor, and Alan Watts. Along with my personal practices I began a propaganda campaign to retrain my brain (my Ipod and Computer were working overtime in this...) I RARELY took breaks from it because I found my first real moment of peace from Eckhart's book, so for me that was clearly my "way out." Everywhere I went there was the voice of someone speaking this material to me and every so often some little gem would spark relief (a momentary Satori) which would give me enough energy to keep going, etc. My meditation was Inner Body meditation with some breath meditation (not yours a much simpler version.)

How did you eventually wake up consistently feeling normal or did it just "happen."

It happens slowly, but only began for me when I stopped resisting the process. I went to sleep at night and instead of begging for my dreams to change (they were REALLY horrible for me) I said "Ok, show me what you think is so damn important..." and allowed it fully... When having no expectation that I will wake holding the evening's peace, it was a much more smooth transition, and, though it may have been a placebo, it seemed the morning after I started "surrendering" to it, I woke up a little less in pain...

I can't seem to get back there for the last 24 hours lol - It's quite frustrating.

You will never go back. That moment is gone, let it go. There is only this moment, this breath, and the peace comes from this moment. Stay with it, it will return when it's time.

Another Right Hemisphere practice that you might want to try while sitting in a cafe for instance would be trying Jesus' "Love thy neighbor as thyself." Just sit and project love and blessings to everyone around you, do it silently in your head. See them as you and give them your full heart. Hold nothing back when you do so and see what happens (reading this might make your angry Left Hemisphere go "No f**king way man!" so that would be a good pointer! lol)

It's coming, you've had firsthand experience for a brief moment that we're not selling you a bag of goods here. lol

Peace is your natural state and you touched it briefly, trust that you will overcome this faulty wiring and get back to your birthright.

Namaste,

Mark

Male (Age 17)

Satsang With Male (Age 17)- Letter 1

hi there im writing to you asking for help. i feel i have no purpose in life and without purpose theres nothing for me left. please help me

Answer

Dear Male (Age 17),

Purpose is a slippery slope. It's a game played by only half of your brain, but it's the half that has been wired to be your primary perception vehicle. Purpose is that desire to look into an unknown future and see something that will make you happy. Something that will make you whole. It's a dangerous game to play because the future never arrives, and yet, we keep playing the game of "purpose" in the only place that ever exists, the present moment. So, how will purpose ever satisfy anyone when the future never arrives? If we always need a purpose (looking ahead as the idea of purpose) and the future NEVER comes, this is a formula for perpetual dissatisfaction, suffering, and nihilistic pain. It's time to take the carrot on the stick away from you and be here now. Change your purpose to this moment, this breath, the breeze that just blew across your face, the tree outside with the birds in it, the sun shining, the face of a smiling person (smiling because you're smiling at them, try it!), and the many many other pleasures that exist just because we do and the OTHER HALF of your brain is designed to do and see just that and only that. It doesn't worry, it doesn't fear the future, it doesn't plan, it doesn't judge, it doesn't analyze, it doesn't make up stories about life and watch them in your head, it IS life. And we as a society have trained ourselves to lose touch with the living perception. It's time to get it back!

I want you to watch this, it's only 11 minutes so it should be easy. It will give you the groundwork you need to begin this discussion with me.

http://www.youtube.com/watch?v=dFs9WO2B8uI

I am here Male (Age 17). I am more than willing to talk with you and work with you, however we need to make one thing clear. I can't DO a thing. Not one thing. I can only point back to YOU and you have to be brave enough to go where I'm pointing. And that will be back to you, to the you that would not need one OUNCE of advice, because you will be living every moment, breathing every moment.

That video will be the start of our dialogue if you are interested.

I wish you peace and grace my friend, namaste.

Mark

Male (Age 17)- Letter 2

thanks mark, had to watch that a few times as it was alot to take in. Female (Age 21) sent me a link for a video called "Deceptively Simple" which i enjoy. did you make this?

im feeling much better now but i keep going threw stages of depression. i have watched alot of eckhart tolles videos and many others. but its so hard when you in a society where people think im crazy.. im 17 and my parents disagree with my beliefs they think i should get a job and shut up basically.

I am still very confused about love also. Is what i feel hormones?? what is love. how would i know.?

many thanks

Answer

Male (Age 17),

Yes I made "Deceptively Simple" but not the video that I gave you to watch. Eckhart Tolle will be a great ally in this, don't let go of him and in fact get a copy of "The Power of Now" and read it over and over (it's an assault against that which causes depression and suffering, so read it even when you think you "know all the material" over and over!)

Parents can disagree with your life choices all they want, but they can't live your life for you, this is YOUR journey. And remember, they too are just products of the environments they were born into. They are giving you the best advice they have out of love. There is no need to fight with them, just love them, they are doing the best they know how.

As for society I will quote Jiddu Krishnamurti:

"It is no measure of health to be well adjusted to a profoundly sick society."

And this society we've found ourselves in is the product of a certain kind of thinking, one that is dominated by only half of our intelligence as human beings (the Left Hemisphere of our Brains), and it has some very painful drawbacks:

Suffering

Alienation

Competitiveness

Smug/Self Righteousness

Fighting

Certainty of Beliefs

In Group/Out Group behaviors

Seeing the world as a bunch of little "objects"

Creating narratives of fiction in our heads and believing them to be true

And the worst:

A dead and lifeless universe full of certain concepts that do not promote life…

It's no wonder people walk around looking like zombies and prey upon each other to make themselves "feel better" or "more important."

If you weren't seen as "sick" by this society I would be VERY worried about you…

But you are here. You are asking profound questions at your young age, that alone is astoundingly rare and amazing.

Don't give into the darkness when that which is calling you is the light itself and you will find that that light is YOU. A "you" that you have not learned to harness because of the way that this society was built and the way that schools are taught and behaviors reinforced. But, nonetheless, it doesn't take from the fact that HALF of your brain is dedicated to seeing the world as an alive, vibrant, love filled place where you not only belong but are a part of everything. One with everything. And EVERY great religious Saint and Figure has been trying for thousands of years to say this very thing. Christ had two laws for instance:

1. Love God

2. Love your Neighbor as Yourself

How many Christians, in the western world which was supposedly created with a Christian worldview, follow these two rules?? Many will claim to follow the first (without knowing what it means) and I've met none who follow the 2nd. Notice Christ gave no exceptions to either, he didn't say:

"Love your Neighbor as yourself if you like how he acts today"

Or ANY parameters at all for how your neighbor deserves your love.

So what were Christ, Buddha, Muhammad, etc. talking about!?

Well as it turns out they were talking about the kind of perception that we all naturally house in the Right Hemisphere of our brains, and that due to our artificial and unnatural environment we have lost touch with.

And it's time we get it back....

Now to begin with, so we have grounds to discuss further, I want you to watch some more of my videos:

http://www.youtube.com/watch?v=_o80Q4pLvTE

http://www.youtube.com/watch?v=kv7H2mFgKt4

http://www.youtube.com/watch?v=DB_WkwPCVl8

http://www.youtube.com/watch?v=wGl2tmB9XVE

http://www.youtube.com/watch?v=PTZDNKHf8M4

This will do for now, there are others, but this will give us a basis for a dialogue. Also I would like you to try to track down, on top of Eckhart Tolle's "Power of Now" I'd like you to find a copy of Dr. Jill Bolte Taylor's "My Stroke of Insight"

Now, it's up to you my friend. I can only point the way YOU have to walk the path.

There is light and life, and it is you. You just need to remember how to BE it.

Namaste,

Mark

Male (Age 17) - Letter 3

thanks once again mark. i will watch the videos you have suggested. and get back to you. i have already seen the quote by Jiddu Krishnamurti when i watched the zeitgeist.

and i have the power of now audio book and listened to it a few times. its really long but good and requires alot of attention. Could i ask What you believe in? (god)etc

also i watched some on communication by marshall rosenberg and how we use violent language to try and get what we want. right and wrong, good and bad, punishment and reward. there all the same game and they are not effective. would you agree?

many thanks

Peace and Love.

Answer

Male (Age 17),

Marshall Rosenberg is talking about the dialogue of the Right and Left Hemispheres and as such is very relevant to the material. How you approach others is an important part of how we view the world.

SATSANGS (Q&A WITH VIEWERS)

My beliefs are pretty clear in the videos I gave you, but if you are still interested further there are a few other videos of mine that discuss religion specifically:

http://www.youtube.com/watch?v=vVkaS-uyIPI

http://www.youtube.com/watch?v=09vWXQgXn6o&feature=related

http://www.youtube.com/watch?v=voAB_9BYc44

These were not on the list of the ones I sent you yesterday but if after viewing all this material you still have questions about my beliefs we can discuss it further.

Namaste,

Mark

Male (Age 17)- Letter 4

Mark can i ask you if you have a family, wife etc. reasons why i ask is because i really try to think that this love thing is effective between a man and a girl. but i see how unhappy people are with eachother. there is only a short time of happiness. what are your views on love with a person for the opposite sex. im really stuck trying to work out why i feel how i do about others. and why i cannot be with a girl to long as i question the reasons and figure out its mostly a game of controlling one another to find themselves to feel secure.

its like people marry etc because they feel this is the way to "make" them happy.

thanks mark sorry if its abit personal

Answer

Male (Age 17),

When you're young it seems as though all your problems will be solved through external sources. We look to careers, spouses, friends, entertainment, children, etc. to make us happy. The realization that there is no external source that is responsible for our happiness is the beginning of genuine insight. Very, very few people at your age have ever seen this clearly. There are literally billions of other voices that will try to sell you on the opposite fact, but it's clear when inspecting this world they've created that they have no idea what happiness is. In the 20th Century alone man was the cause of death of hundreds of millions of people through conflict, that doesn't count deaths due to poor driving because of bad concentration skills, murders, etc. It is a low probability that you, at this age, will see this clearly. It often takes people most of their lives to even glimpse this truth and begin to look outside of their families and jobs and finally to themselves for happiness. You have a rare opportunity to see this now. My answer to you is it simply doesn't matter if you have relationships with anyone, what matters is that you learn how to use the brain that you've inherited through birth. If you do, and very few people know how, then all your relationships will take care of themselves as you will have the infinite patience it takes to deal with egoic and unconscious people.

"its like people marry etc because they feel this is the way to "make" them happy. "

This shows you see the truth of this, if only a glimpse. Joy comes from within not without, but it takes work to see this first hand.

If you want to see how relationships work with egoic people I suggest this video

http://www.youtube.com/watch?v=V3miuaOWsj8

There is no joy to be had in any external sources, joy comes from within, and to feel it you have to learn how to access it, even when we feel joy in a situation it was because we allowed ourselves to feel joy, not because the external source caused it. This is very hard to see at your age, but it's possible through practice and direct experience.

Never apologize for asking questions, for as we are all one, it is merely you asking questions of you. I am more than happy to be here for you, I hope this response spoke to you.

Namaste,

Mark

Male (Age 17)- Letter 5

Mark,

I have seen this many times by eckhart but i watched it again. hehe. i understand or atleast i have a insight into what he is saying. i try not to allow myself close to women as i feel it only brings me pain in the end. such an illusion. but to be blunt i feel the need for sex. so i find it hard to keep away. i know exactly how i will feel during the relationship. to start with its so good but i soon question the feeling. i find it hard to be with anyone as they go with me for external things. its like i cannot have a conversation with women as they can only speak about such silly things. i think im ahead of my age. as my friends and previous girlfriends have there idea of a perfect like with a job house and kids. i dont see myself going this way. i will learn as much as i can and then maybe a monastery.

many thanks mark

Answer

Male (Age 17),

There is no need to go to a monastery, YOU are the monastery. When you learn to allow everything as it is, with no concepts or beliefs layered over it it won't matter what anyone is saying any more or what they like or dislike, they will be perfect as they are. All ideas and concepts come from within you and are given to you by your Left Hemisphere's cataloging and evaluation functions. Most of the beliefs we hold as "ours" are usually just either positive or negative reflections of beliefs given to us by our cultures, parents, and environments in general. None of them are who we are, and none of them are important enough to cling to. Once you let go of ALL of your concepts and abide fully in the present moment there will no longer be need of asking who or what or how anything need be done. This runs contrary to EVERY other thing you will hear in your culture and so sounds "wrong" and in fact, ONLY direct experience will validate this for you. You have to do the work, there is no amount of "thinking about it" that will get you closer to it. Spirituality IS practice, the thinking is just delaying out of fear. Be here now, fully, and watch as your mind struggles to try to distract you from the present moment and back into its clutches, its certainty, the illusion it feeds you to keep you lost and constantly questioning what is. It's a trap that I can't more strongly suggest you see through, and it's up to YOU to do the work. No one else can do it for you.

It's not about learning, it's about doing the work.

Namaste,

Mark

Male (Age 17)- Letter 6

But soon i will have to go down the root of jobs family and things as we need money to live. how do you live.

SATSANGS (Q&A WITH VIEWERS)

Answer

Male (Age 17),

It's not hard to eat and keep a roof over your head in our cultures, that is just a distraction, that is your Left Hemisphere trying to use fear to make you look anywhere but at it and what it's constructed. No job will be "terrible" no house will be "unlivable" none of these evaluations will be of any importance whatsoever once you've done the work. You will no longer wish to stand out or be special in any way. And the answers to how to take care of yourself will be obvious and simple. That thought is just a distraction, just a way that the Left Hemisphere throws fear at you to keep you feeling separate and alone.

And there are plenty of other fears that you can cling to to get out of doing the work. If you want excuses and fears and arguments then your current way of looking at the world is perfect. Keep it, it's fine for that. It also will cause pain and suffering for yourself and others, but that is the trade off. You get to fight, argue, be superior to others, but in return you and they must suffer. In time you will find out that no fear or argument is worth staying in the prison of that worldview and you will be able to drop it without arguing every concept that it can muster to keep you from doing the work. And there is no end to them. You can send me thousands of e-mails with arguments against doing the work:

What about a family?

What about politics?

What about fame and fortune?

What about a career?

What about world hunger?

What about World War III?

etc. etc. etc.

There is no end to this game, you can play it your whole life. Most people do. After 30 or so years you MIGHT begin to see that it's not worth playing, you might...

The REAL question is, why aren't you doing the work now?

What excuse are you using to avoid doing the work now?

What argument is worth pursuing that is worth the suffering it causes?

Namaste,

Mark

Singular Questions

(not from a series of letters)

Male (age 23)

I'm feeling extremely screwed   I have no one to talk to but you, I looked up how much it is costs to buy a car - I'll have to wait for months before I can afford one without credit, I'm in the middle of nowhere where the weather is painful and everyone is egoic and doesn't really give a shit about me, I'm egoic, so I don't care about anyone - it's f**king terrible

Answer

All those evaluations are feeling very true and very serious right now. And my response feels like it's NOT taking it seriously, because I don't.

That is my freedom, not to take evaluations seriously. I make that choice in my life and that IS MY FREEDOM. "Screwed, alone, f**king terrible, middle of nowhere, painful weather..." it's all your evaluations and they're all negative. If you don't stop feeding this part of your brain no one will. You have to tell it you're not listening anymore, or it will continue to feed on you until it convinces you to kill yourself again. It's time to stop listening to it, it DOES NOT have your best interests in mind. In fact IT DOESN'T CARE ABOUT YOU it just wants more blood and more oxygen. Give it problems to evaluate and it feeds. Give it things to complain about and it feeds. Give it this moment, where there is NOTHING attacking or hurting you, and it's got nothing. Unless you feed it when it gives you aches and pains (in response to your presence to see if it can get you out of it) by resisting the aches and pains. It's SO past time for you to stop feeding this thing. If you evaluate this reply of mine, you feed it. If you dismiss this reply, you feed it. If you argue this reply, you feed it. If you listen to it tell you how terrible things are, you feed it. If you think about how terrible things have been in the past, you feed it. If you think about how terrible things will be in the future you feed it. I think it's had enough, it's time to PUSH IT away from the dinner table. Only you can do that. You have my deepest love and compassion and if I could take this burden from you I would, but I can't. STOP FEEDING IT!! IT'S KILLING YOU!! No more chasing methods and hoping that Buteko, or good posture, or a full head of hair, or a change of city, or a change of job, or ... will "cure you" they won't. The only way out is to STOP FEEDING THESE BRAIN FUNCTIONS! Or you will have more of the same. Simple, direct, science. I love you Male (age 23), the Male (age 23) that's alone behind that torture chamber. The one with the big heart and love that's crushed under the machine of that high priority status oxygen sucking machine. Come out and smell the air, hear the sounds, taste the food, touch the textures of this wonderful world. It's time to tell the Story Teller to step off the stage.

All my love,

Mark

Female (Mid 30's)

Hi Mark, was wondering if you suffered high anxiety in the past and if you had any advice regarding this...

Answer

I suffered from depression which was fueled by an idea that the future was meaningless. So, my view of the future wasn't fear, but disgust. Anxiety is a "fear" of the future in some way. It's a way for the Left Hemisphere to keep you "feeling separate" and therefore keeping the blood flowing in its direction. Fear is driven by the Amygdala (found in the Limbic System, or lower brain) and it gets first crack at incoming stimuli, which means that if it hijacks the experience you won't get another shot at it until it reaches the upper brain. And when it does, it ALREADY IS. However, at that point, you are able to "deal" with it. The way to deal with Anxiety is to allow it fully (it already is, so resisting that it is just feeds it.) I'd start with "I feel anxious, and that's ok..." and feel that "ok" FULLY. Then find the anxious thought, idea, belief, experience, and Forgive it fully, it is a product of conditioning. Then Accept (and experience) what is NOW fully. Afterwards, Release it from you, it's just a feeling, it's not YOU. And then Relax, which means access the peace circuitry in your brain through some method (meditation, feel the inner body, follow your breath, focus on your present moment sensory input, etc.) If you complete those four steps with the most sincere energy you should come to great relief. That is my advice, I hope it speaks to you. Namaste.

Female (Age 52)

How do I drop my role as a mother if I am still parenting children?

Answer

You had no need of the role to become the mother in the first place. You are a mother. You don't need a role, or a conditioned set of behaviors to make you one. The moment you agreed to parent the child, you were its mother (notice I didn't say the moment you got pregnant, parenting makes a parent, not biology.) When you allow the role of mother to get in-between you and your child you no longer see them as they are. You now see a "daughter" or a "son" instead of the individual form that they inhabit. When in your role you lose your ability to love, for to love is to accept another as they are completely and with your whole heart, and instead of them being who they are, and you being who you are, you have placed this artificial mental construct in the way called "mother" and "child." And you behave accordingly. More than likely your behavior is merely a reflection either in the positive or the negative of what your mother did (e.g. either "I'll never be like my mother..." or "mama always said life was like a..." etc.) Well, your mother is not in this relationship. Your child is not you. If that worked for you and your mother, then wonderful, this is now. Be here now. Drop the role and see your child as they are, and from that acceptance will spring action that fits the REAL circumstances of your relationship with that individual human form. Otherwise, you are just "play-acting" a mother, be you, you are already a mother, now just release them from the role of "child" and interact in a natural way. There are no roles needed here. In that real space, where you are you and they are their true selves, real love will arise, because in order to see them as they are, you have to accept them as they are, now.

Female (Age 47)

What are your thoughts on manifesting things into your life? Like what if I wanted to manifest a car to drive to and from my job into my life how does that work?

Answer

You are the universe. You have no limits. Of course, as such, you in your true state are also not limited by your beliefs, ideas, and concepts. You get on your knees and you beg the universe for a car. Weeks pass and you do not get the car. In fact, the job that you thought you wanted the car for is lost because you cannot make it to work on time. You look back up at the universe and ask "Why?"

Well, you didn't want to get to work on time, or you would have asked the universe for that, which is NOT the same as asking for a car. Because the manner in which you getting to work would have appeared would have been in line with the necessities of your current path. And that might not be a car. Maybe a friend's daily commute suddenly changes and passes by your place of business each day and you and they are meant to have a meaningful conversation that changes both of your lives one morning on the way into work? You didn't ask to get to work on time, so you didn't get that, you asked for a car. But, remember, you in your true form are not limited by your concepts, ideas, and beliefs. You asked for your concept called "car" but the universe heard what you really asked for, you really asked for the JOY and FREEDOM you thought would accompany the obtaining of the car. And so, immediately it manifested the freedom by releasing you from your job. It then set you down the path to true joy, by creating a limit situation (following the loss of your job, your world crashes around you and forces you to question your beliefs) that ultimately becomes a portal to you finding true joy by letting go of your conditioned ideas of reality. You asked for freedom and joy, and the universe heard you. Were your eyes open enough to see the gifts? Of course, if you resist the opportunities the universe handed you to have true freedom and joy, you could willfully go about getting another job and wishing again for a car, who knows, maybe the next time around you'll see the gifts you asked for as they appear in your world? If not, fear not, the Wheel of Samsara will spin again and you'll get another shot at it...

SATSANGS (Q&A WITH VIEWERS)

Male (Age 34)

In your story about the two sages your "Left Sage" warns against being a failure. You say it's a lie. Isn't it important to have success in this life?

Answer

I'm going to craft my answer to you in the form of a short story, I hope it speaks to you:

The Quiet Life of Desperation

We get sent into the world to "make our way" and dangled in front of us are two enticements that will make us happy and fulfilled and they are: accomplishments and family. We trust those who went before us and take their words, for we've never played the game, so what do we have to compare it to? We find a mate, and for a moment it meets the expectations, we settle into a job and we give it all we've got. We start a family and one of us stays home to watch the children, and the other gives all they've got to their career. We'd played the game with full trust, we went to school and conformed in all the ways it demanded and now we're going to "pay our dues" and climb that company ladder. It takes awhile, but in time we begin to move up. We envision that the higher we go on that ladder the more fulfilling it will be. We hold in our minds this idea of the happy, free, and powerful executives that go golfing and hand all their work to their secretaries. The real job, however, becomes one of greater responsibility. Instead of looking after the lives of your spouse and your family you now have to be accountable for the lives of those under you at the company. At first, it's somewhat manageable as your crew is smaller. But more and more your day consists of solving other people's problems, and you spend less amount of time with your family due to these duties but the money increases so you tell yourself that it's all going in the right direction. Until, of course, the next promotion. The number of people you're responsible for increases again, you have less and less time for yourself, and virtually none for your family, but that's ok because now your spouse spends all their day dealing with the demands of the three children you created together. Your days consist of a mountain of calls from people who are certain that their needs are more important than your time, but that's the job you took! Now, comes another promotion, and now you're lucky if you see your family at all. That's ok, because when you get home your spouse has collapsed into a sleep coma and you crawl into bed next to them and pass out. The intimacy is the snoring they emit all night which keeps you from falling into a deep sleep and your exhaustion builds. The stress is overwhelming and, then one day at work your secretary shows you some kindness. They notice that you're suffering and they offer you the slightest humanity and you realize that you've missed that and you immediately fall in love. You are certain that this person is the answer to all your problems. You divorce your spouse and you quit your job and you "start a new life" but as you do so, you spend most of your time dreaming of your ex-spouse and your family. The second marriage doesn't work out, and you run back to your first. You reunite and "begin again" but the trust is gone now so the marriage isn't the same. You look back at your idea of the executive's life and remember that you wanted freedom and happiness. You both take up hobbies and try to relax and find peace and happiness in your lives. Peace and happiness are, of course, both feelings that come from within you. It isn't until that moment that you realize you've been looking in the wrong places your entire life. You've been looking for external sources to generate internal states. After many many lost years of looking in the wrong direction, you finally turn within. Why not cut out the middle man and learn how to be happy and peaceful directly?

Male (Age 62)

You seem to vilify the Left Hemisphere in this book, is that your intention?

Answer

I mentioned at the beginning of the book that this was not a "brain book" but a book about "liberation practices." This is an important distinction. For, as it turns out, what we need liberation from are the many pitfalls and painful conditioned behaviors that arise when we hand the navigation of our lives over to the narrow and separate feeling Left Hemisphere. It's simply not made for that task. The fault is not with the Left Hemisphere but with the misguided sources that foster and reinforce that worldview. Aggressive and fear-based cultures that cling to the idea that we all have to be "on guard" at every moment in order to survive. That there are "adversarial others" that need to be resisted and feared. And, this worldview has spread through very prosperous and aggressive cultures and continues to grow like a virus. Nature has shown that aggressive species do indeed have some evolutionary advantages, but nature has shown even more often that cooperative species are also (often much more) prolific and successful. The cooperative species (and cultures) are also more prone to longevity. Why? Because while aggressive species rise fast, in the end their aggressive tendencies begin to turn upon themselves when there are no longer "others" to prey upon. So, in the end these aggressive systems are "eaten from within" by their own destructive tendencies. Darwin mentioned the phrase "survival of the fittest" in his works but it has been completely misunderstood over the many years to be equal to "survival of the strongest (most dominant.)" The term "fit" in Darwin's usage does not mean the same as in the term "physically fit" it is used in the context of "the perfect fit" as in one that is most appropriate to the environment it resides within. So, Darwin was not using the term as a salute to aggressive and dominant species, he was using it as a description of the reality that only those species that are best fit to the needs of the environments in which they reside will thrive and therefore continue. So, I ask you, what will best fit the needs of this species that is now so successful that it has surpassed the 7,000,000,000 population mark? It's time to re-adjust our approach and find the best "fit" for the environment in which we find ourselves, and I'm referring of course to the environment that exists NOW. Not hundreds of thousands of years ago, but now. And the evolution that must occur to make this shift happen can no longer be left to external factors, it must come from within. If we are intelligent enough to see all this, then that very intelligence needs to be used to our best advantage. However, once we have righted this imbalance, the objective isn't to eliminate the Left Hemisphere completely. If you had damaged your right leg and favored your left leg while it healed, upon the healing of the right leg you would not then favor the right leg, you would return to a balanced gait, and utilize the tools in the way they were intended. That's what we're attempting to do here, bring our brains to the Buddha's "Middle Path" and no longer ask of our Left Hemisphere that of which it was not meant to do. It's a wonderful tool, and it has the best intentions, but it simply is being used for the wrong task. It was never intended to pilot the ship, it is our navigator, it highlights potential obstacles in our way, it's not nor has it ever been intended to be our pilot. Until we adjust our worldview, it will continue to generate suffering until, when there is no longer any external source to feed upon, it turns back on itself, because it must feed, and it doesn't care where it comes from. So, again, I will quote Dr. Stephen Hawking who cautioned:

"...our genetic code still carries selfish and aggressive instincts that were a survival advantage in the past..."

The past is gone, and liberation from those selfish and aggressive instincts are no longer realities we can ignore if we wish to survive as a species.

Female (Age 48)

If I am responsible for my perception and you are responsible for yours and they both exist, what happens when yours and mine conflict?

Answer

The answer to this will sound paradoxical, if not outright wrong at first, but the actual answer is there are no other perceptions but your own. Only you get to experience this universe through the energy that has manifested into your form and it's a one time performance of a show with a single audience member. And nothing else but your experience occurs filtered through that form. If you perceive that I have a conflict with you, then it is only real because you perceive it as real. Even if I tell you that you and I are in conflict, my assertion does not manifest the conflict unless you accept it. For instance, think of the many masters in history, and what they would respond to that assertion. Gandhi is told that he is in conflict with the British government, and he says "No, there is no conflict, I love you, AND I will not obey you. There is no conflict at all." Or Christ or Buddha turning to the person with love and compassion only in response to anything they generate. If the other form determines the truth of the encounter through their behavior then these responses would be impossible. Think of it as if you were playing a 3 dimensional video game called "you" where you get to pick and choose your responses in the video game and enjoy or fight against what you encounter in the game. Now, by example, if In the middle of a computer video game the phone rings you can pause the game and prioritize the phone over the video game, and more often than not people do just that. They CHOOSE to prioritize the phone over the stimulus coming from the video game. In exactly the same way we have a choice every moment in our life to prioritize peace, joy, and love over any other perceived experience. We can choose one over the other and through that choice we offer the result of that choice to others. There was nary a shot fired (at least not in a formal declaration of war) and the British government simply walked out of India, this choice would never have happened if Gandhi didn't offer it by his own behavior. By choosing to experience the British government from a space of love and friendship he allowed them to finally leave in friendship. That choice came directly from his choice in prioritizing peace and love over conflict and violence. We all have the choice to press the pause button on our 3-D video games called "me" and remember to prioritize peace, joy, love, and harmony over other perceptions and through that share that choice with the world.

Female (Age 56)

I am experiencing some physical challenges when I wake in the morning. Adrenaline shoots through my body and wakes me throughout the night so I wake often feeling tired and groggy. I fear the implications of these health issues and I sit and ruminate about them over and over. My anxiety is paralyzing me and making me afraid to even get up in the morning.

Answer

It's important to separate the physical challenges we face from the "problem solver's" self created stress and strain. The Left Hemisphere sees all challenges as an opportunity to feed. My father's recent death brought out a resurgence of my problem solver's attempts to regain control. "But, Mark, your father just died!" it would urge "Tell me of a greater problem than that!?" it would ask and I would reply "It is not a problem, it just is. Now I must grieve, which is also not a problem..." Even when we suffer from health issues, it's important not to add the problem solver's stress and angst on top of them. In fact, by allowing it completely and doing simply and directly what needs to be done you reduce stress in your life and greatly improve your body's ability to fight off the challenge to its health. NOTHING is an excuse for the Left Hemisphere to enter and start ruminating or stressing, no matter how powerful and seemingly convincing an argument it generates in favor it itself. Remember, there is one and only one scenario the Left Hemisphere cannot see during its rumination phases. It can conjure up hundreds and thousands of possible futures and frightening scenarios. You can pull out one possibility and replace it with another and do so for hours and hours on end, but the ONE thing you will NEVER actually generate with this process is what actually happens in the future. That is the one guaranteed scenario that it WONT see. So, exactly of what use was the rumination? Forgive your body for having the issues it has. Allow the situation fully. Release yourself from its problems, and relax into you, into this moment, no matter what it contains, fully. Much love.

SATSANGS (Q&A WITH VIEWERS)

Female (Age 22)

I've been reading a lot on the debate about the use of chemicals in the treatment of depression and bi-polar disease. I wonder what your take is on the use of medication for people suffering from those illnesses.

Answer

There is no easy solution. You see, what is most often missed in these debates, is that the majority of psychiatric problems stem from poor coping mechanisms in the patients. They, having no effective way to cope with stress, anger, anxiety, etc. feed those brain processes to the point that they are out of control and in the short term only flooding the brain with chemicals will control the behavior. Over all, without learning how to "do the work" and cope with environmental stimuli in a more healthy manner, we can just as easily exchange bipolar disorder and depression with garden variety alcoholism, sex addiction, and entertainment addiction. All of these states are ways for brains who have been abnormally developed due to the over use of certain brain functions to cope with the painful states that those brains generate. In the end, it's painfully simple if one has no way to deal with incoming stimuli in an even and tempered manner, the degree to which they are unable will dictate how ultimately dysfunctional the brain of that person becomes. Greatly unable to handle painful stimuli = greatly dysfunctional, in the many forms that it takes (many of which would never even be mentioned in a psychiatric sense because the people are still able to hold a job and pay taxes and are therefore "sane" by psychiatric standards.) In the end it's simple, like food and bodily health, in the brain healthy input leads to healthy output.

Disclaimer

"Work done with selfish motives is inferior by far to the selfless service or Karma-yoga. Therefore be a Karma-yogi, O Arjuna. Those who seek the fruits of their work are verily unhappy."

- Bhagavad Gita

My biggest concern in the creation of this manuscript is the karmic splash it will make in the universe. Once it leaves my hands it will have a life of its own and it will be beyond my control. I personally believe this work will have little or no major impact on humanity as a whole and know that it will go where the universe guides it in terms of need. However, in case this is the only expression of mine that you, the reader, come across I want to make certain that the following is clear:

1. I am not special

2. I have nothing that anyone else does not have and claim no authority over others

3. My words are NOT authoritative, and not to be used to enforce any belief systems or used to do so by human or non-human "authority figures" whatsoever.

4. I do not sanction or wish created any groups that lay claim to this material as dogma, and do not wish any groups to gather together in the name of this material with the single exception of groups that gather so that the individuals in those groups may work together to better understand the material to do the individual work that the material demands.

5. No one has a right to speak for me or represent my work or use it to demand behavior of another.

6. I want to again assert that I claim the right to disagree with any and all of the material in this book at a future date if I find that further evidence has shown it to be false in my experience.

Copyright © 2012 - Mark Pifer, All Rights Reserved

Printed in Great Britain
by Amazon.co.uk, Ltd.,
Marston Gate.